Market Analysis and Valuation of Self-Storage Facilities

Readers of this text may also be interested in the following publications from the Appraisal Institute:

- *The Appraisal of Real Estate,* 12th edition
- *A Business Enterprise Value Anthology*
- *Convenience Stores and Retail Fuel Properties: Essential Appraisal Issues*
- *The Dictionary of Real Estate Appraisal,* 4th edition

Market Analysis and Valuation of Self-Storage Facilities

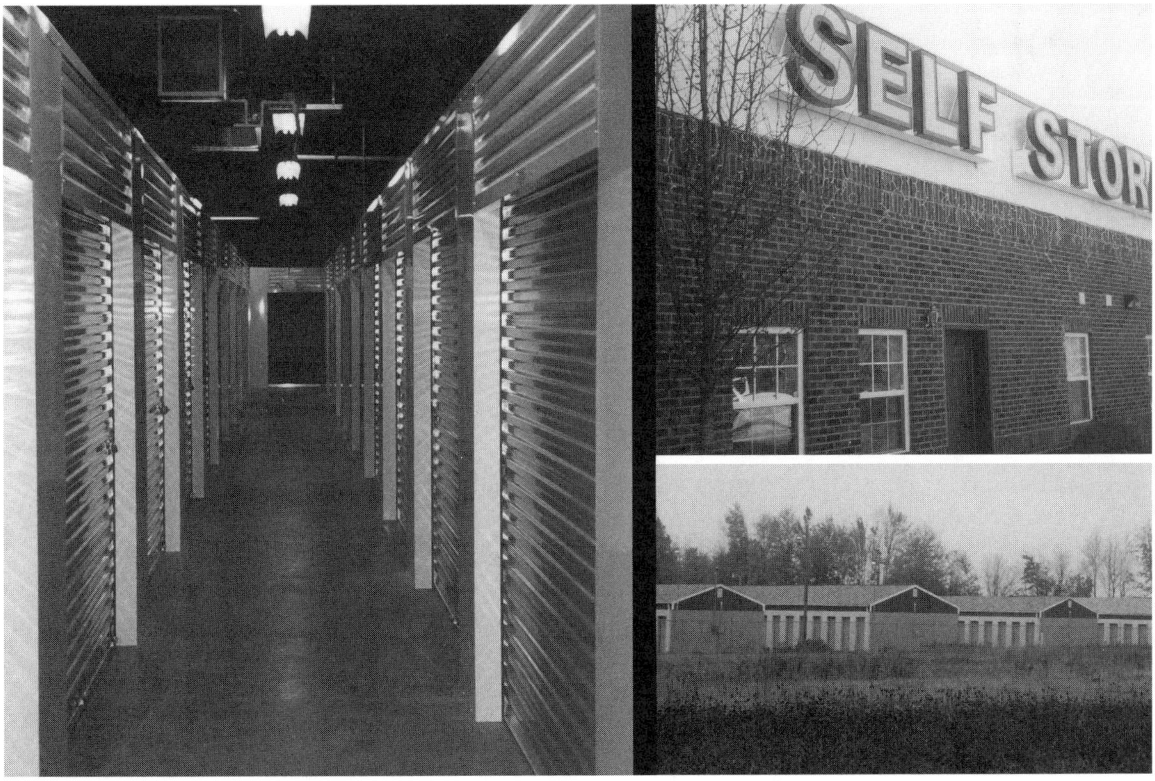

by Richard R. Correll

Reviewers: Frank E. Harrison, MAI, SRA
John A. Kilpatrick
Kelli K. Kline
Vice President, Educational Programs and Publications: Larisa Phillips
Director, Publications: Stephanie Shea-Joyce
Editor: Mary Elizabeth Geraci
Manager, Book Design/Production: Michael Landis
Production Specialist: Lynne Mattick-Payne

For Educational Purposes Only

The material presented in this text has been reviewed by members of the Appraisal Institute, but the opinions and procedures set forth by the author are not necessarily endorsed as the only methodology consistent with proper appraisal practice. While a great deal of care has been taken to provide accurate and current information, neither the Appraisal Institute nor its editors and staff assume responsibility for the accuracy of the data contained herein. Further, the general principles and conclusions presented in this text are subject to local, state, and federal laws and regulations, court cases, and any revisions of the same. This publication is sold for educational purposes with the understanding that the publisher is not engaged in rendering legal, accounting, or other professional service.

Nondiscrimination Policy

The Appraisal Institute advocates equal opportunity and nondiscrimination in the appraisal profession and conducts its activities in accordance with applicable federal, state, and local laws.

© 2003 by the Appraisal Institute, an Illinois not for profit corporation. All rights reserved. No part of this publication may be reproduced, modified, rewritten, or distributed, either electronically or by any other means, without the express written permission of the Appraisal Institute.

Printed in the United States of America

Library of Congress Cataloging-in-Publication Data

Correll, Richard R.
  Market analysis and valuation of self-storage facilities / by Richard R. Correll.
    p. cm.
  ISBN 0-922154-77-5
    1. Self-storage facilities–United States. 2. Market surveys–United States. I. Title: Self-storage facilities. II. Title.
HF5487.C65 2003
381.4'56488–dc22

2003058341

Contents

Foreword vii

About the Author viii

Preface ix

Chapter 1   History of Self Storage 1

Chapter 2   Self-Storage Site and Building Characteristics 5

Chapter 3   Market Analysis 11

Chapter 4   Valuation Methods and Techniques 33

Chapter 5   Case Study: Proposed Falls River Self Storage 49

Foreword

Self-storage properties are found in rural, urban, and suburban areas throughout the United States, but many real estate professionals and market participants simply do not understand the dynamics of the self-storage market. *Market Analysis and Valuation of Self-Storage Facilities* has been developed to describe the operation of this volatile market segment and to educate appraisers and others about the value of existing and proposed self-storage projects.

Self-storage assets have characteristics of both industrial and retail properties. Operators and investors in self-storage facilities must cope with intense management requirements, erratic rental patterns, tough competition, and rapid fluctuations in demand. Appraisers and analysts can help them meet these challenges by providing better feasibility studies and adopting new methods of market analysis in their appraisals.

Market Analysis and Valuation of Self-Storage Properties provides readers with a reference text and a framework that establishes a new level of analytical sophistication for this asset class. This publication will give appraisers greater knowledge and new insights into self-storage facilities, which will allow them to provide owners and investors with more refined analyses that will contribute to better business decisions.

Alan E. Hummel, SRA
2003 President
Appraisal Institute

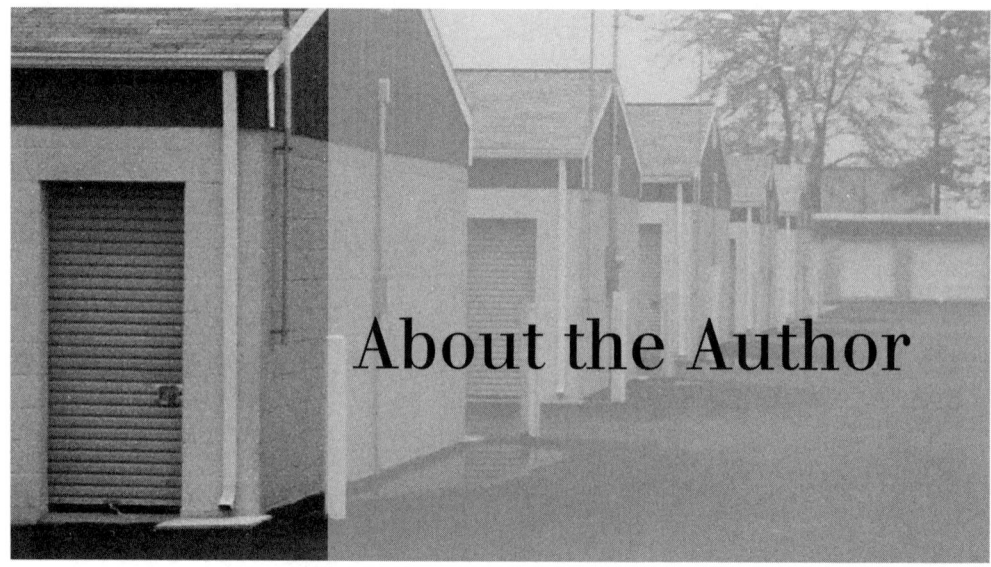

About the Author

Richard R. Correll is the president of Correll Commercial Real Estate Services located in Indianapolis, Indiana. For more than 17 years, Correll has been an appraiser and consultant working to provide national, regional, and local clients with a variety of real estate solutions, including market studies, feasibility analyses, valuations, brokerage services, counseling, and litigation-related services.

Preface

We live in one of the most prosperous countries in the world and our rate of consumption as individuals and households far exceeds that of most countries on the planet. Americans accumulate many things and we have become an increasingly transient society since the 1950s. While much of our purchasing is consumed or disposed of, some of it is saved and fills our basements, garages, sheds, and attics. Combine a consumer society with the trend toward more densely designed residential communities and stricter outdoor storage restrictions and you have the foundation for self-storage demand. The demand for storage and the proliferation of self-storage facilities has been a constant, if not explosive, proposition over the past 40 years.

The Storage Explosion

The 2000 U.S. Census reported that the U.S. population was approximately 281.5 million. At the same time the total amount of U.S. self storage was estimated to be approximately 1.3 billion square feet, indicating that there were approximately 4.62 square feet of self-storage space for every person in the United States. As a comparison, the U.S. population in 1960 was approximately 180.6 million and there was an estimated storage supply of only 180 million square feet, or approximately one rentable square foot of self-storage space per person. The trend is clear. The amount of self storage per person in the United States has quadrupled in the past 40 years.

Storage as an Investment

The evolution of self storage from an industrial-type asset to a more sophisticated retail-like investment asset has helped the industry expand the definition of personal and business storage in America and the world. Now that storage has earned a place in the real estate investment universe, having demonstrated its ability to survive economic cycles and be embraced by Wall Street investors, it should be treated with the same analytical sophistication as other real estate investment assets. Unlike real estate investment sectors such as office and retail property, the self-storage asset class is not supported and scrutinized by an army of third-party leasing brokers and management groups. Self storage is still a homegrown asset and a specialized investment class. However, the dramatic expansion of storage and individual property financings has led to total U.S. debt commitments on self-storage properties of more than $30 billion. Of course, this amount is still small when compared to commercial property debt. A Mortgage Bankers Association survey indicates outstanding U.S. commercial property debt of more than $1.78 trillion. Storage debt accounts for less than 1% of U.S. commercial real estate debt, but that number is growing and the average debt commitment on storage assets is also increasing. While national players are in the self-storage field, the self-storage business is still considered a "mom and pop" industry. This means that good advice is always welcome in the property development and financing processes.

The Need for Knowledge

The self-storage market is more volatile than many other sectors, and many appraisers and others simply do not understand its dynamics. Month-to-month leasing, the impact of new supply, reliance on external demand generators, and management intensity all make analysis and forecasting difficult. Combine these challenges with an investment market that is managed by a handful of brokers, with most transactions occurring between principals, and the stage is set for a difficult analytical process. If appraisers have difficulty, so do market participants who may include a local developer who is seeking a new opportunity and a retiree

> Market participants who are new to self storage may have a lot of optimism and view the endeavor as a gateway to easy wealth. This attitude changes once they begin to realize how competitive and transient the business can be. A self-storage operation needs good marketing and management. The best "mom and pop" facilities have managers/owners who work long hours and are committed to every detail of operations, from customer interaction to picking up trash on the property. Since this industry has so many independent operators, the sophistication of management can vary widely.

who is making a long-term investment. These participants may not understand the market, but they have no problem finding turnkey building providers or sites that are available for development. These projects may be ill-conceived but they always find their way to a financing source. With the market so heavily populated with projects, we need better feasibility analysis and a new approach to market analysis.

This book will appeal to commercial appraisers and other real estate professionals who desire a better understanding of the analysis and valuation of self-storage facilities. It contains real-world examples and step-by-step instructions that can be applied immediately and are not available elsewhere. The book was written to educate appraisers about practical methods for the valuation and analysis of existing and proposed self-storage projects. Some of the techniques are intended to challenge existing standards and explore concepts that result in more refined results. The case study in Chapter 5 shows how those methods are employed.

The self-storage industry has many participants, including developers, brokers, investors, appraisers, lenders, managers, and community officials. This book is addressed directly to the commercial real estate professional, but the techniques and methods discussed here will interest a wide audience of self-storage industry participants. The ideas, advice, and instructions on market analysis presented, for example, will help developers uncover more development opportunities and avoid costly mistakes. Readers should be familiar with basic commercial real estate valuation concepts and with self storage as an established, but newer, real estate investment.

Some traditional methods of analysis and valuation are explored and updated here to meet today's information-intense market. The use of computers, advanced appraisal techniques, and sophisticated market analysis concepts raises the bar for practitioners and creates a better basis for understanding the industry.

The chapters in this book will lead readers step-by-step through the analysis and valuation of self-storage facilities.

- Chapter 1 discusses the history of self storage, providing a basic understanding of this asset class along with background on the institutional investment market.
- Chapter 2 explains the physical and locational components of self-storage projects.
- Chapter 3 shows how to organize and structure a market analysis.
- Chapter 4 discusses valuation approaches and techniques.
- Chapter 5 is an actual case study of a proposed project.

Finally, this book was developed out of a desire to educate professionals on methods of analyzing existing and proposed storage projects. The large number of storage projects that now exist and the varying locations and configurations of facilities make sophisticated analysis important. With the rising tide of storage supply, it is clear that there will be winners and losers in the years ahead. For those who can identify opportunities and avoid pitfalls, risk will be mitigated; less nimble market participants will likely suffer. Many believe that self storage is the key to instant wealth or a vehicle for diversifying more narrow investment portfolios. Several national companies provide an all-too-positive outlook on self-storage performance rates. My goal is to provide a reference text and a framework that establishes a new level of analytical sophistication for this asset class and allows industry participants to make more informed decisions.

Chapter 1: History of Self Storage

Between 1996 and 2002 more than 300 million square feet of new storage supply, with an aggregate value of more than $12 billion, was added to the U.S. self-storage market, increasing the total U.S. supply to nearly 1.3 billion square feet. Given this growth, there may never be a better time for greater knowledge and improved methods of analysis. By the end of 2002 there were nearly 35,000 self-storage facilities in the United States.

The first self-storage projects were developed in Texas in the late 1950s to meet the needs of migrant oil workers. The product then migrated to Sunbelt regions throughout the 1960s and 1970s, but as late as 1975 the industry was still considered to be in its infancy. One writer that year wrote, "The new and exciting world of mini-warehouses can be built anywhere in the country to fill a vast untapped demand."

By 1989 a great deal of this demand had been filled and oversupply, combined with the beginning of a national recession, decreased the euphoria of the previous decade. At the end of 1990 there were 174 self-storage facilities with a combined book value of $190 million on the inventory of properties to be disposed of by the Resolution Trust Corporation (RTC). These numbers were an early indication of bad times for self-storage facilities. Even so, the total book value of all RTC properties at that time approached $18 billion, so self storage was a small portion of the total.

> In 1972 only 104 self-storage facilities in the United States were advertised in the Yellow Pages.

The savings and loan debacle of the late 1980s and the economic recession of the early 1990s precipitated a credit crisis. Suddenly, healthy companies with performing portfolios were unable to borrow needed funds from traditional sources for acquisition and expansion. For the self-storage industry this was a brutal reality since all self-storage projects are speculative and there is no pre-leasing activity. The tight credit markets set the stage for real estate investment trusts and commercial mortgage-backed securities to fill the capital void created when traditional capital sources withdrew from the self-storage market. (Real estate investment trusts [REITs] are investment vehicles that combine the capital of many investors to finance real estate. Commercial mortgage-backed securities [CMBSs] are backed by loans secured with commercial property.)

Wall Street investment and the emergence of strictly economically viable projects became the trend in the early 1990s. The Wall Street pundits promised a new era of real estate ownership, accountability, and discipline. It was thought that public markets would immediately react to market conditions and bring discipline to the historically unwieldy commercial real estate industry. REITs have proven to be active acquirers and developers, establishing an institutional market for self-storage real estate. The friendly relations between old-line real estate companies and Wall Street turned somewhat cold later, however, as storage executives felt the immediate and ruthless impact of stock and capital market pricing. In mid-1998 an investor retreat from REITs and a shift in capital pricing slowed aggressive acquisitions.

A study of the industry reveals that from the beginning self-storage facilities struggled with their identity, a fact epitomized by the variety of names that have been used to describe them, including

- Mini-warehouses
- Mini-storage
- Mini-storage warehouses
- Self-service storage
- Self storage
- Self-storage mini-warehouses

Today the most widely used term seems to be *self storage*. In the next decade facilities will probably be identified by brand names such as Storage USA and Public Storage, which will bring to mind an established product and array of services. The Internet will continue to strengthen brand recognition and allow storage users to find facilities from coast to coast.

Self Storage as an Institutional Investment

The 1990s was the decade of the real estate investment trust (REIT). According to the National Association of Real Estate Investment Trusts (NAREIT), in 1990 there were

119 publicly traded REITs with a market capitalization of approximately $8.7 billion. By July 2003 there were a total of 173 REITs with a market capitalization of more than $185 billion. Table 1.1 is a summary of REITs by property sector.

Table 1.1 REITs by Property Sector (July 2003)

Sector	No. of REITs	Market Capitalization (in Billions)	% of Total
Industrial/office	36	$52	28
Retail	35	47	25
Residential	25	31	17
Diversified	18	15	8
Lodging/resorts	16	7	4
Health care	13	9	5
Self storage	3	6	3
Specialty	7	8	4
Mortgage-backed securities	20	10	6
Total	173	$185	100

Source: NAREIT

When combined, office, industrial, retail, and residential REITs constitute more than 70% of the total value of all REITs. Within the self-storage sector, there are only three REITS, with a market capitalization of approximately $5.8 billion, or 3% of the total market capitalization of all REITs. The market capitalization of the largest REIT, Public Storage, is larger than the other two combined, as shown in Table 1.2.

Table 1.2 Storage REITs—July 2003

Symbol	Name	No. of Facilities	Market Capitalization (in Billions)	Capitalization per Facility (in Millions)
PSA	Public Storage	1,397	$4.2	$3
SHU	Shurgard Storage	475	$1.2	$2.5
SSS	Sovran Self Storage	260	$0.4	$1.5
	Total	2,132	$5.8	

Source: NAREIT

The 2,132 storage facilities owned or managed by REITs represent approximately 6% of the nearly 35,000 self-storage projects within the United States.

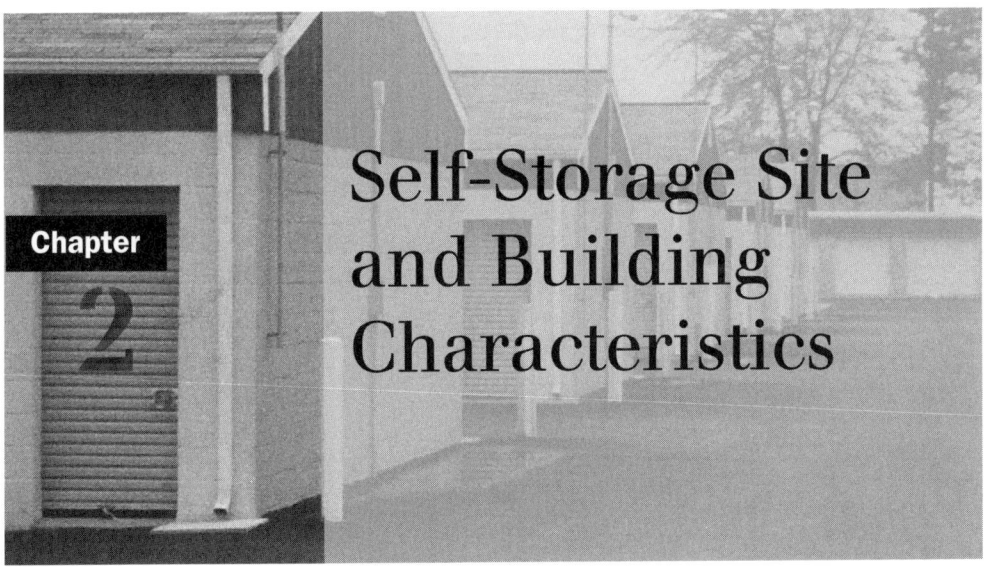

Chapter 2

Self-Storage Site and Building Characteristics

Site Characteristics and Trends

As storage projects have evolved in sophistication and market acceptance, they have increasingly been built on higher-priced land. It is not uncommon for storage projects to be located along retail corridors and adjacent to residential districts. Most new suburban projects are located on sites with good access and visibility that are convenient to users. A typical suburban or rural storage site may be very deep or flag-shaped with minimal frontage for access. Site size varies, but two to five acres is common with the building covering 40% to 50% of the site area. Visibility is essential because more than 50% of storage business is generated by drive-by traffic; the remainder results from advertising. The site configurations shown in Figure 2.1 are typical.

The flag-shaped site is common. Such a property has good access and visibility but is positioned off of the frontage land, which usually means a lower land cost. Furthermore, a rectangular site that is divided in this way may preserve the front section for an outlot use. There are many reasonable locations and configurations for self-storage sites. In hilly areas, projects can be designed to work with the topography. It is not uncommon to see a project with ground-level access and an elevation variance of 20 to 40 feet.

Industry experts believe that convenience to the population base is essential for a project's success. Consider a new 60,000-sq.-ft. facility located off a major

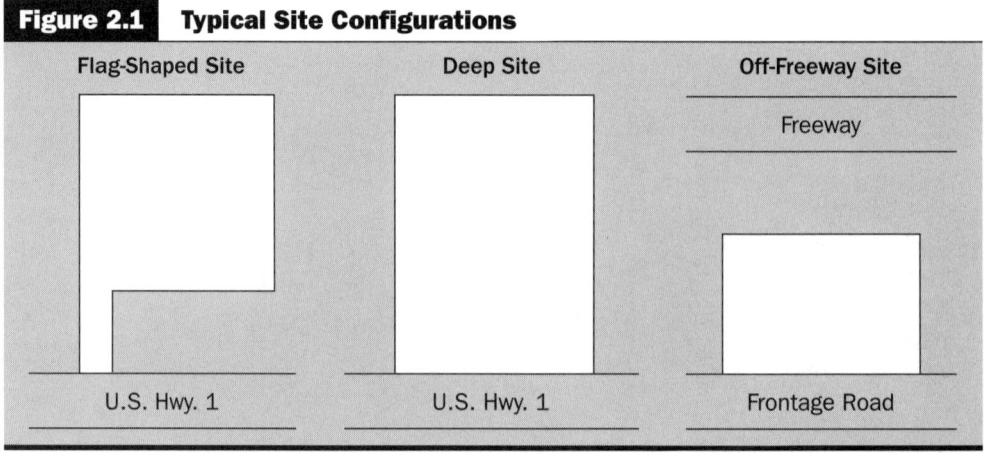

Figure 2.1 Typical Site Configurations

freeway between two towns that are 30 miles apart. The facility has good visibility and access, but it is not very convenient. Most users would be required to drive to the facility as a "destination" that is 10 to 15 minutes away. Based on industry statistics, this is the maximum distance a user will travel for storage space. Thus, even though this facility has good access and visibility, its lack of convenience could hinder the project's success. Slow lease-up is one of the major risks of a self-storage development. Sites that have a good balance of accessibility, visibility, and convenience are most likely to compete successfully.

After several years of favorable economic conditions in the United States and a tremendous amount of new development in all real estate classes, local zoning authorities and government bodies continue to tighten the building code requirements for proposed self-storage projects. Requirements for building design, quality, landscaping, drainage systems, fencing, density, and fire code regulations, which were already restrictive, seem to be increasing. As self-storage projects move closer to retail and residential districts, better landscaping, fencing, and building facades are generally being required.

The increasingly difficult process of obtaining zoning approval has lengthened the development timeline. While self storage is not viewed by community officials as harshly as projects such as manufactured home parks, it is still not highly regarded by many municipalities.

Many industry participants believe that a maximum project size of 80,000 square feet has the best operational return. According to the principle of decreasing returns, adding more square footage to this optimal size will lead to decreasing returns. Although 80,000 square feet is considered the threshold amount for a single-story suburban facility, plenty of projects that are much larger will do well, especially if they are multi-story facilities.

The optimal site size can be determined based on building area. The size of a self-storage site can vary from one to 15 acres. A site size of two to five acres is typical for suburban projects. In most locations, local zoning requirements will allow a maximum building coverage of 50% of the site area. An 80,000-sq.-ft. project built at 50% building coverage would require 3.67 acres (160,000/43,560 square feet). In practice, most existing facilities are much smaller, especially rural projects, which tend to be smaller than self-storage facilities in urban and suburban locations. In 2002 the average size of a self-storage facility in the United States was 35,039 square feet.[1] This is the size of a typical "mom and pop" project.

Building Characteristics of Self-Storage Properties

When evaluating properties, access to the facility and access to individual storage units are primary considerations. Since self storage is generally used by transient residential users, building spacing must allow an adequate turning radius for moving trucks. The facility layout can also enhance the property's curb appeal and the overall utility of the site. Figure 2.2 shows various building configurations.

In most projects, buildings should be spaced 30 feet apart to allow for loading and access. More than most types of investment real estate, self storage has embraced sophisticated technology. The newest facilities are equipped with high-tech security, automated access, and utility systems. They also exhibit strong design elements, including appealing color combinations and a creative use of materials. Today's facilities offer a wide array of unit sizes and typically include some climate-controlled space, specialized storage for recreational vehicles or records, and perhaps even upper-floor space.

Property Reuse/Adaptive Reuse

Many properties can be converted for storage use. The costs to convert a property may compare favorably with the cost of an existing improved property, making reuse financially feasible. Old urban commercial structures may be converted into vertical storage, or industrial/retail-type buildings may be converted into indoor storage. A more unusual reuse is the conversion of an old underground mine into storage space. The availability of custom-configured building systems makes many conversions viable.

The public acceptance of hybrid-type storage projects is mixed. A converted-use property may have more difficulty renting space. Typical self-storage projects

---

1. *Self Storage Almanac 2003* (Phoenix: Minico, Inc.)

Figure 2.2 **Typical Improvement Configurations**

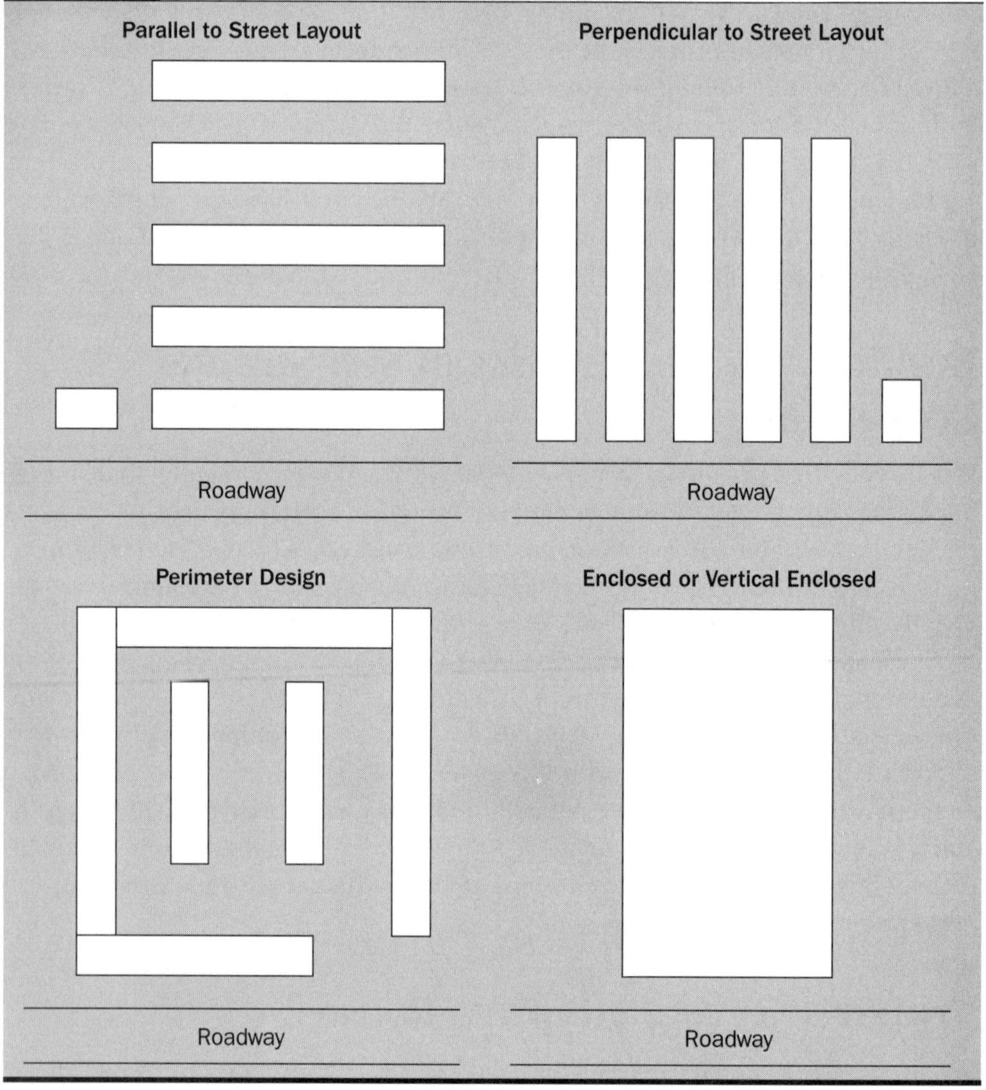
Parallel to Street Layout
Perpendicular to Street Layout
Roadway
Roadway
Perimeter Design
Enclosed or Vertical Enclosed
Roadway
Roadway

are familiar to storage users. A converted project is less common and its management may have to try harder to attract users and traffic.

Climate-Controlled Space

The term *climate control* refers to space that is heated, air-conditioned, or humidity controlled. More than 17% of all self-storage facilities in the United States offer climate-controlled units,[2] compared with only 11% of facilities in 1997. The increase

2. Ibid.

in climate-controlled space is driven by two factors: the demand for this space by residential customers and the property owner's ability to charge more for it. The amount of climate-controlled space in projects will likely continue to increase in the years ahead.

Multilevel Facilities

Nearly 10% of all self-storage facilities in the United States have multiple levels.[3] The highest concentration of these self-storage facilities is in the Northeast, where 25% of all new facilities are built with multiple levels. In most markets, second-floor space is more difficult to rent than first-floor space because the units are not as accessible. Also, providing elevators adds expense and liability for the owner. The advantage of multilevel storage is higher project density. The performance of upper-level space is driven by local market characteristics. In some markets, upper-floor space is perceived to have increased security and will rent for a premium.

Storage projects in proximity to retail and residential districts generally have higher land costs. During the late 1990s developers successfully developed quality facilities in convenient locations. This has put pressure on existing facilities in inferior locations. Often a new facility captures a large share of the market, producing marketwide occupancy shifts and a net loss for older facilities. This market phenomenon is common in other classes of investment real estate such as office and retail properties. The next wave of storage development has yet to occur, but it may involve some of these innovations:

- Mixed-use storage projects
- Physical storage uses for technology and data storage
- Higher service revenue
- Joint ventures with feeder organizations such as moving companies

REITs have been very proactive in developing business plans to ensure strong occupancy rates for properties in their portfolios. They commonly engage in joint ventures to attract business or develop products.

> Within the United States, multilevel facilities are becoming more common and their development is driven, in part, by a desire to place more building area on smaller parcels. Multilevel facilities typically have large cargo elevators that lead to upper-floor storage units. Storage users have accepted these facilities, but not in all market areas. Some market participants have a "park in front and load" mentality, which means that multilevel facilities will have to prove their viability against conventionally designed competitive space.

---

3. Ibid.

Facility Design and Construction Trends

Most self-storage facilities are constructed from steel or a combination of steel and concrete block. The overall quality of the steel used for storage development has improved. Older facilities built of weaker grades of steel or wood depreciate rapidly.

Within the United States, the majority of self-storage facilities are constructed out of prefabricated metal. Some facilities have been built using masonry materials such as brick and concrete block and some wood facilities still exist. The most recent trend in construction is the use of manufactured steel components that are assembled on site. Often the exterior appearance of a self-storage facility is dictated by local zoning codes.

Chapter 3

Market Analysis

Any type of real estate analysis involves fundamental market analysis because value is influenced by the price of competitive properties. The relationships between the price, quantity, and desire for a particular type of property are all aspects of real estate market analysis. Self storage is interesting in this regard because the interaction of the market forces of supply and demand is very clear and direct. The problems associated with the economic recession of the early 1990s reminded real estate investors and developers that market research and analysis could help mitigate risk. While fraud and lending abuses contributed to real estate problems during the recession, the proliferation of supply in the face of decreasing demand reminded participants that real estate is a cyclical investment with periods of prosperity and decline. An imbalance between supply and demand continues to plague self-storage investments and reflect the fragmented nature and inefficiencies of supply delivery in this market segment.

> "We are seeing tremendous oversupply all over the country."
> - A self-storage investment analyst

One important goal of this book is to provide readers with a basis for organizing and analyzing self-storage market data to improve their decision-making and analysis. Many appraisers do not devote sufficient attention to market analysis. For many clients, the commercial real estate appraisal has become a service or product driven by price and delivery time. This trend, which is partly the result of the regulatory requirements imposed on appraisals for loan transactions, has limited the time appraisers spend developing and analyzing market data. This is especially true for self-storage market analysis, which requires a substantial amount of fieldwork. As professionals, practitioners must develop skills that adapt to market needs and work to provide solutions to clients' problems. The services provided may include appraisals, consulting, tax appeal, brokerage, or expert testimony. In today's information-intense market, participants seek answers to a variety of questions regarding self-storage facilities.

The income assumptions made in any investment property analysis should be anchored by strong market data. This is particularly true for self-storage projects because effective income volatility caused by shifts in supply and demand can result in poor financial performance. A self-storage property is developed and operated for the sole purpose of generating an economic return that is commensurate with the risk of the endeavor. The primary motivation for an investment in self storage is economic. The acquisition or development of a manufacturing facility may be undertaken to serve business purposes but, in self storage, the commodity is simply various size storage units and open storage that is rented to users on a monthly basis.

Self-storage entrepreneurs, like most real estate investors, are a diverse group. For example, an investor may be a farmer using excess land for a small storage development or the CEO of a self-storage investment portfolio. Both investors need an analysis of market relationships prepared by an appraiser who knows how to complete a detailed market study for existing and proposed self-storage projects.

The design and organization of the market study required depend on the type of assignment and the questions that need to be addressed. The format presented here can be adapted to a large number of assignments, including appraisals, consulting assignments, and research reports. The following outline reflects the organization of this chapter and a typical market study.

1. Industry overview
2. Definition of the competitive market area
3. Identification of the competitive supply
4. Supply survey
5. New supply
6. Supply segmentation
7. Demand
8. Demonstrated demand
9. Tenant mix
10. Potential demand
11. Pent-up demand

12. Supply and demand balance
13. Analysis of rental rates
14. Market position of the subject property

A fully developed market study should identify the market area in which a property competes and assess the relationship between supply and demand at a specific point in time. Such an analysis will consider past trends and the likelihood of future events. While this may seem more extensive than most clients require, the process described here provides a framework for the analysis of self-storage properties and markets. The appraiser may reorder, consolidate, or skip certain steps, depending on the type of assignment and the specific questions being asked, but understanding the procedure and applying the principles discussed here will result in better analysis.

On a macro level, a market study is always influenced by current capital/debt pricing and availability, government regulations, and economic conditions. The state of the economy, interest rates, and government regulation all play key roles in the viability of self-storage projects. On a micro level, the analyst must consider all relevant submarket relationships, including supply and demand relationships, and the existing or proposed position of the subject property relative to the competition. This analysis will involve fieldwork and extensive research.

An industry overview is provided at the beginning of the market study to inform the reader about current industry trends and set the stage for discussion of the subject property. Sources of information may include industry periodicals such as the *Mini-Storage Messenger* and *Self Storage Today*, industry associations such as the Self Storage Association, and industry reports from Wall Street analysts, which can be found on the Internet.

Industry Overview

The self-storage industry is relatively young and has proven to be resilient. Over the past 40 years, the supply and quality of self-storage properties have increased and their locations have generally improved. An overview of the industry might include

- A brief history of self storage
- National industry trends and news
- Macro level supply/demand relationships
- Major industry participants
- Future forecasts
- Financing market

The industry overview sets the stage for the more detailed market study that will follow.

Sample Industry Overview

After a proliferation of self-storage development in the late 1980s and the resulting over supply, the industry re-emerged in the mid-1990s as a feasible development option. This resurgence was driven by a strong economy, housing expansion, good employment, and low interest rates. By 2001 and 2002 the market began to experience the negative effects of ongoing supply additions, which were further complicated by decreasing demand. In 2003 there will likely be less new development and continued industry consolidation.

The storage industry has continued to mature, leading to more sophisticated products and more refined development methods. Several companies offer turnkey storage systems, which allow local entrepreneurs to enter the market with a sophisticated product and an established management system. This has resulted in an expansion of low-quality facilities in mainly rural and suburban areas.

While large investors such as REITs own 6% of the self-storage market, the market is still dominated by small owners, who operate one or more facilities within a local market area. REITs continue to acquire and develop facilities, marking the continuing trend toward industry consolidation.

Within the self-storage market there are several regional and national storage owners: Public Storage, Storage USA, Metro Self Storage, U-Haul Storage, U-Stor, and Shurgard. These companies own more than 2.5 million square feet of storage space within the metro region. This equates to a market share of more than 60%, with the balance of local space owned by individuals. Within this market, national companies such as Storage USA have been aggressively acquiring existing projects. Other participants such as Public Storage have preferred new development. The subject property will be operated as an independently run facility rather than as a franchise of a national chain.

This overview of the industry can be expanded or shortened depending on the use of the report. The main objective is to describe macro level data for this class of property. The next step is to identify the competitive market area in which the specific property (proposed or existing) is located.

Definition of the Competitive Market Area

The market area or "submarket" is the geographic region in which a specific property competes for storage users. The traditional industry method for defining the submarket for a self-storage project is to draw a circle with a three- to five-mile radius around the subject property; the subject property is the center point of the circle. In many situations an analyst using this method, called the *concentric circle approach*, can identify most of the existing or prospective storage users and competitive facilities.

While the concentric circle approach is widely accepted, it may not be accurate in all situations. For example, erroneous results may occur if the subject storage project is located in a rural area immediately off the exit ramp of a major freeway. This facility may have a higher-than-typical reach, with a long but narrow market area extending 10 miles down the freeway. In this instance a concentric circle analysis could be misleading and the analyst should turn to other measures, such as zip codes or census tracts, to adequately define the submarket. Many existing facilities keep records of customer zip codes, which makes mapping the market area relatively easy. For proposed developments this can be more difficult. In any case, the analyst can avoid erroneous results by not using a concentric circle analysis exclusively. Physical barriers such as freeways, rivers, or other impediments to access, which can limit or change the size and shape of market areas, must be considered.

In the United States there are three to five primary market patterns for self-storage facilities. All storage markets are unique in shape but many have parallel patterns. Analysts need to be aware of storage market patterns because such patterns are the foundation of successful analysis and, potentially, indicative of a project's success. The variety of patterns suggests how many storage submarkets have been mapped. Figure 3.1 shows three typical market area patterns. The star in each drawing represents the subject property.

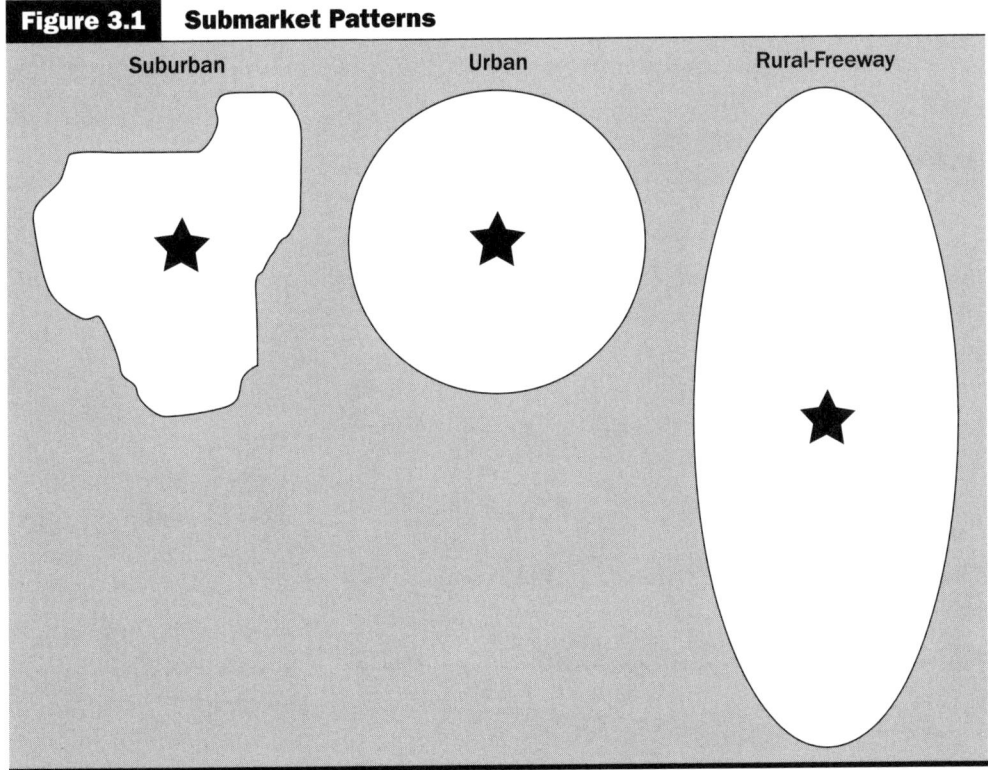

Figure 3.1 Submarket Patterns

In most suburban markets, users will travel a maximum of 15 minutes, and many miles, to reach a storage facility. In contrast, a multistory urban facility may have a market radius of only a few blocks. Self-storage submarkets are uniquely defined. It is not uncommon to find two properties that are located only two miles apart but have vastly different performance rates due to access and visibility, market characteristics, and pricing. Although many owners of existing facilities keep records of tenant zip codes, which can be used to identify the typical market pattern, identifying the market area for proposed facilities is more difficult.

Once the competitive market area has been defined, the analyst must acquire demographic statistics such as current population and housing data for the defined region. These demographic statistics may be based on census tract, zip code area, or the area drawn using the concentric circle method. A concentric circle analysis based on user-defined parameters can be compared to other analyses to refine the results. Several companies offer online demographic data for user-defined parameters (see resources listed at end of chapter).

Defining the Market Area for an Existing Facility

To understand how to define the market area for an existing facility, consider the following example. A 50,000-sq.-ft. facility built in 1981 is located along a commercial corridor in suburban Phoenix. The facility is on a flag-shaped site, with an access road leading to land at the rear that is improved with storage buildings. The site configuration is shown in Figure 3.2.

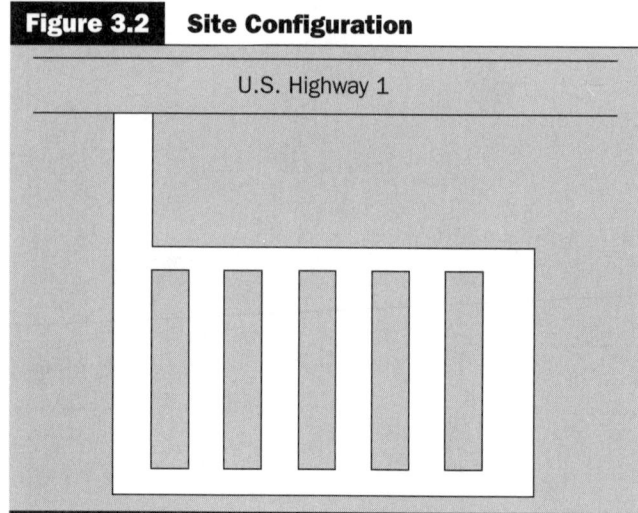

Figure 3.2 Site Configuration

The manager of the facility indicates that 90% of the tenants are residential users and 10% are commercial users. The facility is 95% occupied and the manager has a printout of customers by zip code. More than 80% of the tenants are located in three zip code areas. Some storage bills are sent out of state. Typically, a certain percentage of users are not residents of the market area. Nonetheless, the manager's records provide a starting point for estimating the primary market area. Based on the zip code information provided and concentric circle mapping of a 3.5-mile radius, the market area looks like Figure 3.3.

The primary market area is the region defined by the zip codes (the solid line). It is roughly the same as the concentric circle overlay (the dotted line). Table 3.1 shows the population statistics for the concentric circle and the zip code area.

In this case, there is not much difference between the data for the zip code area and the circle overlay. The estimated current submarket population ranges from 235,000 to 239,000 and is expected to grow to 240,000 to 245,000 over a five-year period. Identifying the competitive market area is essential to a good market study. The market area for an existing facility can be defined using primary data (e.g., actual client zip codes) and secondary data (demographic statistics).

The next step in the study, the identification of the competitive supply, analyzes the subject property's competitors, which can also yield information that helps define the competitive market area. If the market area as defined is not consistent with how properties compete, the practitioner may need to redefine the market area. Each step of the analysis must be consistent with the other steps.

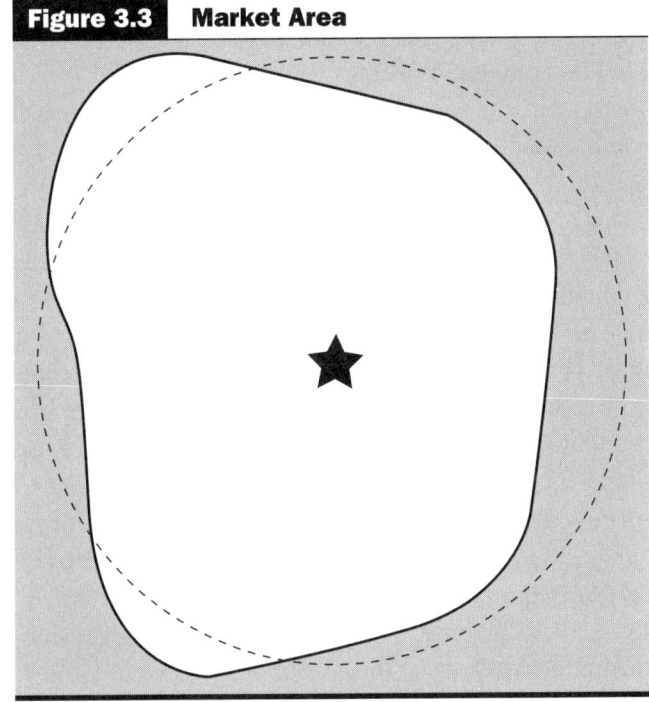

Figure 3.3 Market Area

Table 3.1 Estimated Suburban Phoenix Submarket Population

	2003 Population	2008 Population
3.5-mile circle	235,000	240,000
Zip code area	239,000	245,000

Real estate professionals must understand how markets operate to complete better analyses and improve decision making. The advent of affordable technology and information access has improved the sophistication of technical analysis. When better data is combined with diligent fieldwork and research, a sophisticated analysis of market relationships can be produced.

Identification of the Competitive Supply

The first step in any supply analysis is to identify the properties within the defined submarket and select those that are competitive with the target property. This can be complicated because most submarkets overlap and properties within the defined market area will be more or less competitive with the target property. In fact, some properties within the submarket may not compete with the target property at all due to their location, condition, or storage offerings. The properties that constitute the competitive supply will likely be within the defined submarket area and it is the analyst's responsibility to identify and survey those properties. The characteristics of these properties to be considered include project quality, unit pricing, and location.

Interviewing managers and owners of nearby storage facilities is the best way to identify the competitive supply within a submarket. Analysts can visit or telephone a facility and identify themselves and the nature of their research. Generally owners and managers are willing to discuss the properties they compete with and can provide an informed perspective on how the market is performing. If the property being analyzed is an existing facility, management should be able to identify the facility's primary and secondary competitors. More information can be obtained through interviews at the competing properties, but since storage markets overlap, analysts will likely find it worthwhile to do some research to narrow in on primary competitors. Figure 3.4 illustrates how overlapping storage submarkets might look and how a group of properties might compete.

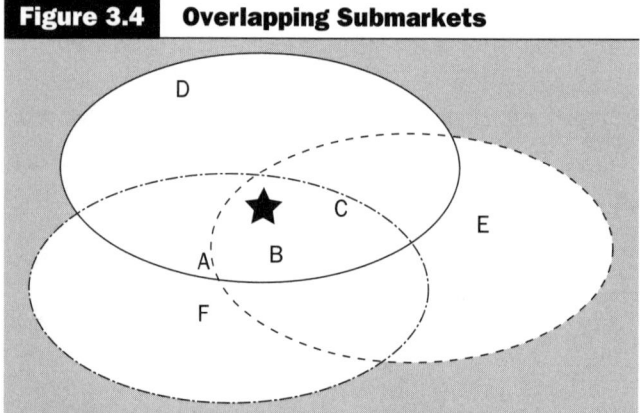

Figure 3.4 Overlapping Submarkets

In this illustration three separate submarket regions are defined by the intersecting ovals. The subject property is identified with a star. Note that properties A and B are within the lower and middle ovals. All the properties shown compete with C, but only A and B compete with E and F. This may sound like a trick math problem, but it simply shows how storage submarkets can overlap and complicate defining the competitive supply. Three conclusions can be drawn from Figure 3.4:

- The subject property competes with Properties A, B, C, and D.
- Property A primarily competes with Properties C, B, and F.

- Property B primarily competes with Properties A, C, and E.

Identifying competitive supply is not a science, but a method for quantifying actual market relationships to increase knowledge and enhance decision making. Quantifying relationships can help decision makers uncover market opportunities or avoid pitfalls. Once the analyst has defined the competitive market area and competitive supply, a map like Figure 3.5 may be drawn. Again, the star represents the subject property and each letter is a competitor.

After identifying the primary competitive supply, which typically includes three to 10 properties, a more detailed analysis of their attributes can be completed and presented in a survey format.

Supply Survey

The supply survey is a summary of all known, relevant facts about competitive properties within the submarket. Opinions, property attributes, and other information can be obtained from a variety of sources, including interviews, public records, and physical inspections of the properties.

Most supply surveys adequately identify occupancy and absorption rates at the time of the analysis, but they are less successful at identifying trends. Since storage is subject to seasonal fluctuations in most regions and is sensitive to external events, the analysis should be extended slightly by trying to obtain both current and past occupancy information. Insight into the trials and tribulations of the submarket over the past year is especially important for proposed facilities because marketwide net occupancy gains are a benchmark of future performance. The inexperienced practitioner will commonly forecast absorption based on the performance of a new facility down the street, without taking into account the fact that the older facilities located farther down the street are experiencing net declines

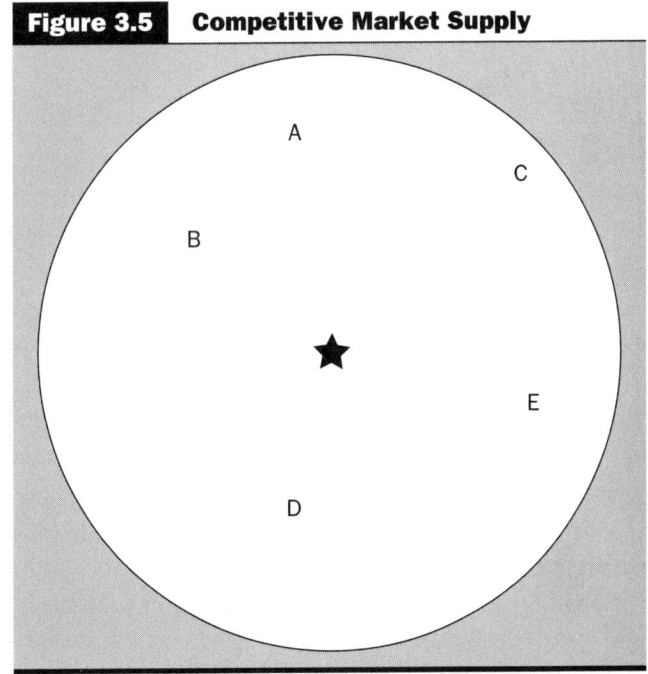

Figure 3.5 Competitive Market Supply

in occupancy. Submarket rate and occupancy trends are better understood when analyzed over a period of time, rather than at a single point in time. Figure 3.6 is a sample survey of one property.

After data on all of the properties has been gathered, a summary of key facts can be presented in a spreadsheet format. From this survey the analyst can extract information on total supply and overall occupancy rates. Before this information can be analyzed, however, the introduction of new supply must be considered.

New Supply

Any study of supply invariably involves consideration of the introduction of new supply. This is especially important for self-storage markets where barriers to enter the market are low and project development schedules are short. The month-to-month nature of self-storage leasing also makes it vulnerable to changes in supply. An analysis of the supply side of the equation always involves consideration of new supply, which may include projects under construction, planned projects, and recently opened facilities. The best way to research new supply is to contact local planning authorities, who should be aware of all new or proposed projects. Planned supply is included in the following sample analysis because it can be very important to the feasibility of a proposed project.

In smaller markets, interviews with managers and owners are usually a good way to learn about new projects. Further study of supply includes consideration of the type and quality of the facilities that populate the submarket. This is called *supply segmentation.*

Supply Segmentation

Not all storage projects are created equal. Over the years the public perception and sophistication of self-storage facilities have continued to evolve. Given that the typical economic life of a storage project is more than 45 years, the early history of self storage is still evident throughout rural, suburban, and urban America.

Self-storage facilities have proliferated in many forms to serve the needs of American storage users. Unlike asset classes such as office buildings, there is no classification system for rating self-storage projects other than those published in well-known cost guides, which generally do not mirror market activity. With a market presence of more than 100 years, office real estate has an accepted system of classifying properties as Class A, B, or C space. This real estate classification system is based on several factors, including building quality, size, location, and age. Building classification is not an exact science, but rather an accepted language for communicating the position of assets within the investment real estate universe.

Figure 3.6 Sample Property Survey

				Rents for	
	Rent comparable	Storage Place		Climate-	
1		1122 Main Street		Controlled	Regular
		Jackson, MI	Unit Size		
	Phone number	255-9087	(in Feet)	Space	Space
	No. of buildings	5	5 × 5	$48	$35
2	No. of units	577	5 × 10	$75	$49
	Year built	1996	7.5 × 10	—	—
	Grade	C+	5 × 15	$88	$63
3	Residential	70%	5 × 20	$98	$70
	Commercial	30%	10 × 10	$110	$76
		July	July	10 × 15	$150	$92
		2001	2002	10 × 20	$175	$118
4	Occupancy	87%	93%	10 × 25	—	$160
	Rent increase/decrease (2001–2002)	0%–+2%	10 × 30	—	—
			10 × 40	—	—
	Construction	Brick	10 × 50	—	—
	Building area (net rentable area)	70,240 sq. ft.	15 × 20	—	—
5			15 × 40	—	—
	Avg. unit size	122 sq. ft.	20 × 15	—	—
	Other space	On-site apt./office	20 × 20	—	—
			20 × 25	—	—
			20 × 30	—	$288
			20 × 40	—	—
			30 × 30	—	—

(Section 6 brackets the Unit Size / Rents columns)

Supply Survey Format

Section 1
This section of the survey identifies the surveyed property by name, address, and telephone number. The telephone number is useful for follow-up interviews.

Section 2
This portion of the survey includes the number of storage buildings, the number of units, and the year the property was built. Properties are graded A through D. This is a subjective opinion that takes all factors into account. The grade differs from the class rating. A Class C facility may be graded B+ within the class. Classes of space are defined in Table 3.2.

Section 3
This shows the tenant mix of the property. It is important for understanding sources of demand and the degree of similarity to the subject property. This information is usually obtained from interviews with managers and owners.

Section 4
Information on current occupancy and past occupancy is not always easy to obtain, but it is one of the most important measurements of the market's vitality. The rent trends over the past year are also indicative of the market's strength.

Section 5
Other building characteristics that can be obtained from public records or observed by driving by the property include construction type, size, and the presence of a management office, apartment, or outdoor storage component. Analysts should add a comment line for additional relevant items such as the condition of the property or the inclusion of excess land.

Section 6
This last part of the survey shows monthly rental rates for each type of unit, including climate-controlled space, if applicable. Some facilities have specialized storage space such as boat storage, which should be accounted for separately.

Market Analysis

In self storage there are differences between facilities; some are better than others, and the best facilities attract the highest institutional investor interest. The classifications shown in Table 3.2 can be used to differentiate the range of property types that exist.

Table 3.2 Self-Storage Facility Types

Facility Type	Description
Class A	An institutional-grade facility with a gated entry, an on-site office and manager's apartment, masonry construction, and sophisticated design and layout. These facilities typically range in size from 60,000 to 120,000 square feet and feature high-tech security, climate-controlled units, and signature design elements. They are located in primary and secondary retail-type locations in major metropolitan areas.
Class B	A quality middle-market facility with a combination of masonry and metal construction. These facilities have an on-site office and sometimes a manager's apartment. The facilities will range in size from 30,000 to 60,000 square feet and exhibit basic design elements. Some properties may offer climate-controlled units and outdoor storage. These properties occupy secondary commercial and primary industrial locations in first-tier and second-tier markets.
Class C	An average-quality facility typically featuring metal-constructed buildings. There may be an on-site office or simply a phone number directing customers to the building management. These facilities range in size from 20,000 to 100,000 square feet and are basic in appearance. They are usually located in secondary commercial, rural, and industrial locations.
Hybrid	Property conversions, vertical applications, indoor configurations, and specialty facilities designed to fill a special niche. Some properties have a regular storage component and a specialty storage component such as a boat storage building.

Classification is intended to help quantify the various types of properties in the market, but properties will always be a mixed bag of characteristics that demonstrate the visions of entrepreneurs throughout the country. A metropolitan area has a wide range of storage alternatives to fill the various needs of the market. Over the years storage projects have become increasingly sophisticated to better meet the demands of storage users.

> "Our business thrives on social and economic flux. When people are changing jobs, residences, marital status, and moving between cities, business is very good."
> – Storage industry executive

Demand

If supply is the skeleton of the storage body, then demand is the heartbeat. The analyst must understand the different types of demand, such as demonstrated demand and potential demand, and how supply and demand information can be combined with demographic statistics to measure the health of storage markets.

Demonstrated Demand

The simplest measure of current storage demand is the performance rates of existing facilities within a competitive market area. This is known as *demonstrated demand* and is estimated based on the occupancy level and amount of space occupied within a submarket. Table 3.3 is a summary of five facilities–four existing and one planned–within a sample submarket.

As shown, occupancies within the submarket range from 94% to 97%, demonstrating a strong demand for storage space. The data indicates a total submarket supply of 230,000 square feet with 60,000 square feet planned, for a total of 290,000 square feet. Although 219,250 square feet of space is occupied, at this point adequate demand to support a new facility has not been established. Before assessing potential demand, the tenant mix of the submarket must be examined to understand where demand is originating.

Table 3.3 Sample Facilities

Facility	Current Occupancy	Size (in Sq. Ft.)	Occupied Area (in Sq. Ft.)
A	96%	60,000	57,600
B	94%	75,000	70,500
C	97%	45,000	43,650
D	95%	50,000	47,500
E (Planned)	0%	60,000	0
Total		290,000	219,250

Tenant Mix

The type of storage users that populate a submarket generally fall into two categories: residential users and commercial users. Table 3.4 is a summary of the national tenant mix by region based on information in the *Self Storage Almanac 2003*.

As shown in Table 3.4, 94% to 96% of U.S. storage demand comes from residential and

Table 3.4 Self-Storage Tenant Mix by Region

Region	Commercial	Residential	Other
Northeast	17%	78%	5%
Southeast	22%	74%	5%
North Central	19%	75%	5%
South Central	19%	76%	4%
West	20%	75%	5%

Based on information from *Self-Storage Almanac 2003*
Percentages are rounded

commercial customers. The majority of this demand, between 74% and 78%, is generated by residential users. A residential tenant is a person requiring extra household or yard storage or someone in the process of relocating. A residential user may be an apartment dweller, mobile home owner, or single-family home owner. The typical commercial client is a sales representative or vending route operator who uses storage to hold products. Many storage facilities permit trade businesses such as painters, landscapers, and contractors to use their facilities. Beyond the two traditional categories of self-storage users, a wide variety of tenant types form the core business of some facilities. These users may include military personnel, large companies, students, automobile enthusiasts, and airport-related storage users.

The type and mix of tenants is unique to each submarket and can be measured by analyzing survey results and evaluating demographic data, but the typical storage project will cater to residential and commercial traffic. For the most part, residential business accounts for 50% to 90% of a typical facility's tenant base, while commercial business accounts for 10% to 50%. Identifying the tenant mix is important to understand the sources of demand for an existing or proposed facility. According to *Self Storage Almanac 2003*, the average tenant mix for U.S. storage projects is 75% residential users, 20% commercial users, 3% students, and 2% military personnel.

Potential Demand

At this point, the market area and the competitive supply have been identified. In the supply survey the analyst has summarized facts about the type of tenants and the performance rates of existing facilities. In the next step, the analysis of potential demand, the analyst brings together demographic statistics, survey data, and professional judgment to quantify potential demand. This step is particularly important in the analysis of proposed facilities. In the previous example, the total existing supply in the submarket was determined to be 230,000 square feet with 60,000 square feet planned for a total of 290,000 square feet. In this example, it will be assumed that the sample submarket is located somewhere in the Midwest. As a starting point, consider the relationships between storage supply and population in several Midwest markets in 1996 and 2001 (see Table 3.5). Figures for selected Midwestern cities are shown along with totals and averages for the top 50 metropolitan areas in the United States. Note that the rentable square feet (RSF) per person is a common industry ratio used to measure the saturation levels of storage markets.

The rentable square feet per person (RSF) is a ratio of population to storage supply. If a defined region has a population of 100,000 and storage supply of 300,000 square feet, then there are 3.0 RSF per person (300,000 sq. ft./100,000 people). Table 3.5 shows that the top 50 metropolitan areas in the United States had a combined average of 3.93 RSF per person in 2001. In 1976 many market participants thought

Table 3.5 — Midwestern Market Statistics

Market Area	Number of Facilities 1996	Number of Facilities 2001	1996 RSF Per Person	2001 RSF Per Person
Columbus, OH	118	177	2.67	4.34
Indianapolis, IN	117	187	2.57	4.39
St. Louis, MO	181	249	2.58	3.63
Grand Rapids, MI	102	123	3.32	4.26
Top 50 metropolitan areas	9,690	12,384	2.57	3.93

Based on information from *Self Storage Almanacs*, 1997–2002

that 1.0 RSF per person was the equilibrium point, i.e., the point where supply and demand would be in balance for most markets in the country. In 2003 a rate of more than 4.0 RSF per person has been reached in the Midwest, and levels of 6.0 RSF per person have been achieved in the West and Southeast without causing substantial oversupply. The ability of storage markets to thrive at supply levels of 4 to 6 RSF per person is a testament to the increased acceptance of the business by users and the evolving sophistication of storage offerings.

On an aggregate basis, storage supply has been increasing faster than the rate of population growth. The RSF per person is a benchmark figure for assessing storage saturation levels in metropolitan areas, but the figures can be misleading. For example, the state of Wyoming has 10.36 RSF per person, which far exceeds the typical Midwest ratios of 3 to 4 RSF per person. At first glance, it may appear that the state has an oversupply of storage space, but further review indicates that there are only 134 facilities in the entire state. Thus, there is probably not excessive supply in Wyoming, but rather a higher ratio of storage space per person. A very different situation exists in New York, where there are 1.68 RSF per person due to high population density.

Application of an RSF ratio is useful and important, but the figures must be interpreted to reflect the relationships within a particular area. Table 3.5 shows that an RSF of 4.0 per person is probably reasonable in the Midwest. Now the analyst must consider the relationships within the sample submarket. Based on research, the analyst extracted the demographic data on population trends within a one-, three-, and five-mile radius of the subject property (see Table 3.6).

Table 3.6 — Concentric Circle Analysis

Area	2002 Population	2007 Population
One-mile radius	20,000	21,000
Three-mile radius	48,000	50,000
Five-mile radius	67,000	70,000

The table shows that there will be 50,000 to 70,000 persons within the submarket (three- and five-mile radii) by 2007. Assuming 4.0 RSF per person and a submarket population of approximately 60,000, potential total storage demand is projected to be approximately 240,000 square feet (60,000 × 4 = 240,000).

The current supply is 230,000 square feet and 60,000 square feet are planned, which will increase a total near-term supply to 290,000 square feet. This number suggests that the submarket may experience a slight oversupply with the addition of the new facility. The analyst should remember that there will be demand for a maximum of 240,000 square feet by 2007. This estimate is based on a submarket drawn using the concentric circle approach. Alternatively, the analyst could have considered population projections based on census tract and zip code statistics. Assume that census tract and zip code analysis indicate that the submarket will have a population of 75,000 in 2007, not approximately 60,000, as estimated using concentric circle analysis. With a future population of 75,000, the total future storage demand would be 75,000 × 4.0, or 300,000 square feet.

A potential future storage demand of 300,000 square feet suggests that the new supply may be in demand or that pent-up demand may be building within the submarket. Ultimately, the analyst must choose the final population estimate by considering the reliability of the source of the data and the likely potential of the submarket. In this example supply will exceed demand, or supply and demand will be in equilibrium. In the mid-1990s markets were recovering and the building boom had not yet started, so there was a shortage of supply in many markets which resulted in pent-up demand.

Pent-up Demand

Any demand that is not satisfied by existing facilities is considered pent-up demand. In a market where occupancies hover around 100% and there are waiting lists for certain types of units, there may be a shortage of supply. The identification of pent-up demand is especially important in the analysis of a proposed facility. Pent-up demand can be difficult to quantify, but the methods previously described can be used to help measure pent-up demand.

The existence of pent-up demand is usually good for proposed facilities, which will likely experience strong initial lease-up and may even develop a waiting list of customers before the project opens. Lease-up activity and absorption rates will vary by facility and the speed of lease-up and absorption will vary with local market conditions. Many market participants refer to rules of thumb indicating a lease-up rate of 2% to 3% per year for a typical 60,000-sq.-ft. facility. Facilities can have net absorption ranging from 500 to 9,000 square feet per month (which should cover just about every facility in the country). The net absorption rate refers to the occupancy of a facility over a set time period, such as a month, quarter, or year. For example, if each tenant rents 100 square feet during a typical month, a facility may gain 15 tenants who rented a total of 1,500 square feet but lose five tenants who vacated a total of 500 square feet. In such a case, the net absorption would be 1,000 square feet.

In estimating pent-up demand, analysts must remember that the absorption rate of a new facility is unique to each submarket and a new facility may capture a significant percentage of new demand, resulting in occupancy loss for existing properties. Many new properties are built in better locations than their competitors. The trend has been to build storage facilities near retail uses on higher-priced land, which are invariably superior locations. The new facilities may do very well, particularly at the expense of older facilities in inferior locations. Thus, a picture of net absorption in a submarket area for a one-year period might look like Table 3.7.

The net submarket absorption of 17,000 square feet indicated does not all represent new demand, which is a common oversight. Clearly, the new facility captured a significant portion of new demand and a substantial amount of existing demand from users who changed facilities. Since storage is rented on a month-to-month basis, it is not uncommon for users to switch to a better-priced or better-positioned facility.

Table 3.7	Net Absorption
Properties	One-Year Net Absorption (in Sq. Ft.)
New facility	+ 25,000
Existing Property A	+ 5,000
Existing Property B	– 5,000
Existing Property C	– 8,000
Net absorption	+ 17,000

Supply and Demand Balance

Industry data seems to indicate that self-storage markets are always being battered by new supply and, at times, overrun with excessive demand. This push-pull process reflects how the asset is leased and the market it serves. A hotel achieves rate and occupancy results based on daily activity, so it could be said that hotel space is rented daily. Apartment space is rented yearly, office space is rented for several years, and retail space is sometimes rented for 20 years. Self-storage space is rented on a monthly basis. According to industry statistics, the average rental period for a residential tenant is eight to 12 months. Commercial tenants typically have longer occupancies, ranging from one to two years.

Residential tenants occupy the majority of U.S. storage space and have the highest turnover rate of any group. The transient nature of residential tenants can be both a benefit and detriment to self-storage performance. On the positive side, rents can be increased to match market conditions. If demand exceeds supply, rents can be increased quickly because tenancies are month-to-month. Conversely, every month the facility loses tenants that must be replaced to maintain occupancy.

The average occupancy levels of U.S. storage facilities ranged from 79% to 89% between 1998 and 2001. While average occupancies appear flat, they do not begin to tell the full story of market activity over the period. Since occupancy is directly related to the rents charged at a facility, national average rent trends are relevant.

Analysis of Rental Rates

Rents for a typical 10-ft. × 10-ft. unit from 1992 through 2001 are shown in Table 3.8 and Figure 3.7.

Table 3.8 Average Monthly National Rental Rates (10-Ft. x 10-Ft. Units)										
Region	1992	1993	1994	1995	1996	1997	1998	1999	2000	2001
Northeast	$67	$66	$65	$64	$66	$65	$71	$68	$71	$71
Southeast	$55	$56	$60	$62	$49	$54	$55	$59	$57	$59
North Central	$45	$49	$44	$47	$48	$49	$47	$48	$49	$51
South Central	$45	$43	$46	$47	$47	$48	$46	$47	$45	$47
West	$57	$58	$57	$59	$58	$57	$65	$63	$61	$67
National avg.	$53	$54	$54	$56	$54	$55	$57	$57	$55	$59

Source: Based on information from *Self Storage Almanac 2002*

As the historical data shows, the rental rates vary by year and geographic location, but the most significant trend is the lack of consistent rent appreciation over the years. In 1992 a 10-ft. × 10-ft. unit in the North Central region had an average rental rate of $45 per month. Eight years later, in 2000, the average rent was $49 per month, an increase of about 9%, or only 1.1% per year. Over the period shown, the average rental rate for a 10-ft. × 10-ft. storage unit in the various regions ranged from $43 to $71 per month. Most regions show rate increases and declines over the period. The erratic performance of the rates can be attributed to the constant pressure of new supply and the transient nature of the majority of demand. The inability to maintain effective rent growth is an important factor to consider when analyzing individual project performance.

As mentioned previously, there is a strong relationship between occupancy and rental rates. In one market study, a particular chain with multiple facilities consistently reported higher-than-typical occupancy rates. These facilities had rental rates that were 10% to 20% lower than comparable competitive facilities. The relationship between rate and occupancy must be understood to forecast financial results.

The analysis of rental rates brings together the information gathered in the survey of competitive supply. The rental rates for specific unit types within a submarket provide a basis for estimating the prospective rental rates of a proposed facility or the

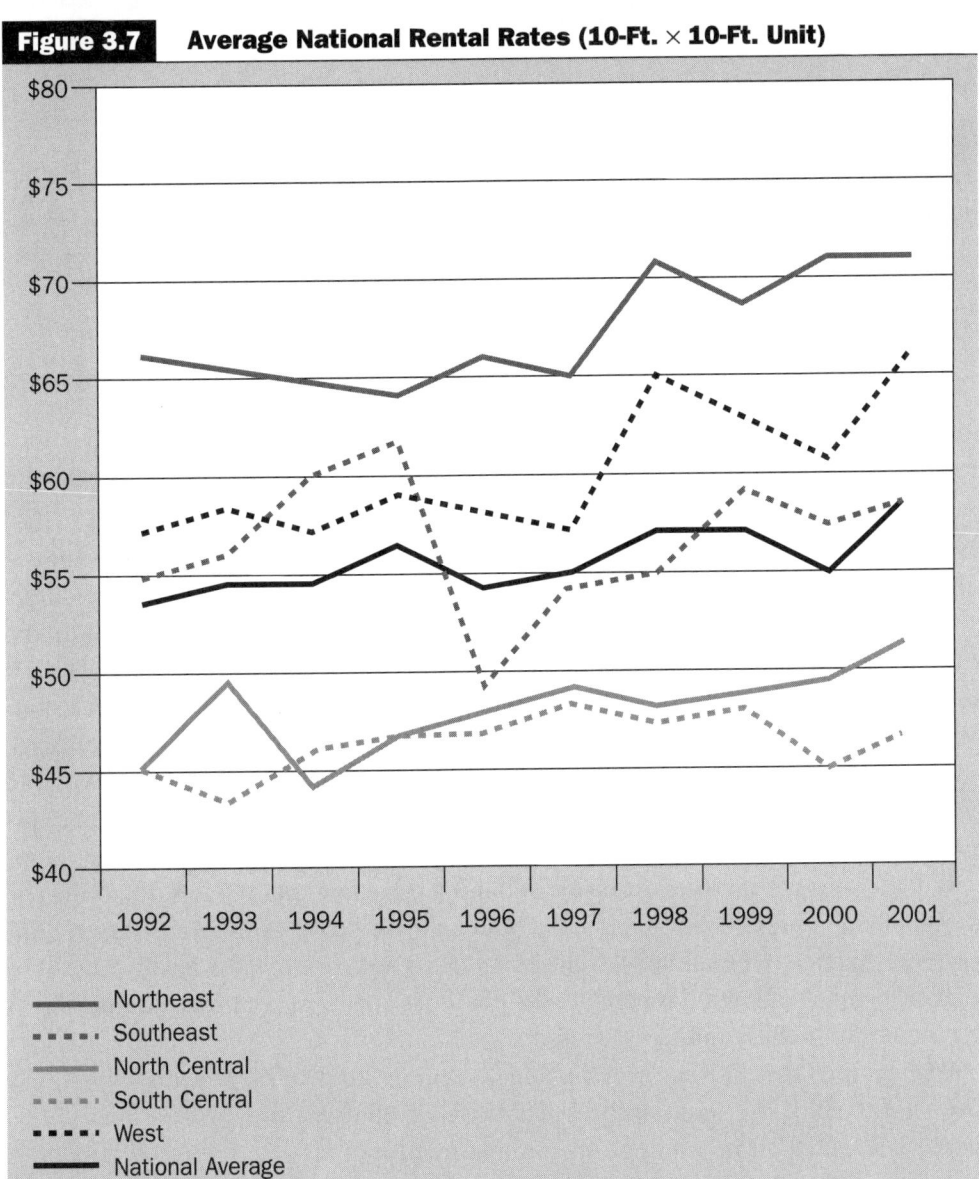

Figure 3.7 Average National Rental Rates (10-Ft. × 10-Ft. Unit)

competitiveness of the rental rates at an existing facility. Analysts should find out if any concessions or special discounts are being offered that could reduce the effective rent. Table 3.9 is a summary of average rental rates by unit type for four facilities.

In many markets, competitive rental rates are analyzed in terms of the rent per square foot for a storage unit of a particular size. When rents are analyzed on a square-foot basis, it becomes obvious that rental rates increase dramatically as the size of the unit decreases. This is especially true for units of less than 100 square feet. Analyzing rent per square foot per month makes it easier to project the economic rent for a particular unit type.

Table 3.9 allows the analyst to compare rental rates by unit type across several facilities. Some facilities will have regular unit types with higher ceilings or odd

Table 3.9 Average Rental Rates by Unit Type

Unit Types (Size in Feet)	Facility A	Facility B	Facility C	Facility D	Average Rent per Sq. Ft.
5 × 5	$33	$35	$30	$35	$1.35
5 × 10	$45	$48	$49	$45	$0.95
10 × 10	$72	$73	$70	$75	$0.73
10 × 15	$90	$92	$89	$90	$0.60
10 × 20	$115	$118	$115	$112	$0.56
10 × 25	$140	$135	$138	$140	$0.56

configurations. If rents are much higher for one type of unit in a facility, the analyst should do more research and find out why. The pricing for similar storage units within a submarket is usually fairly consistent. However, it is difficult to obtain the unit mix at competitive facilities due to the proprietary nature of the data. Thus, it may be difficult to quantify demand by unit type in most situations, but relationships can be inferred based on interview data.

Some managers or owners will indicate that demand for 10-ft. x 10-ft. units within the submarket is high, while there is an overabundance of 5-ft. x 5-ft. units. This information is helpful in ascertaining the overall performance of the subject property. If the target property is proposed and has a large amount of 5-ft. x 5-ft. units, the development plan may be changed to avoid an oversupply. Conversely, it is not uncommon to encounter an older facility with many large units. This facility may have higher income potential if reconfigured into large, medium, and small units. This is an important highest and best use issue.

Given the costs of new construction, including land costs, the pro forma for a proposed facility will likely indicate rental rates that will support these costs and achieve a return on investment. In some secondary markets, the major barrier to entry is an abundance of cheaply priced storage units. These markets may not support a new high-quality facility. It is important for the analyst to consider rates in relation to market phenomena. After giving careful consideration to supply characteristics and the different components of demand, the analyst can form a complete picture of the market.

> Most individually operated facilities have units that are rented to the owners, friends, family, or others who do not pay the standard rate. These units may account for 1% to 5% of the rent roll and they must be identified to establish the credibility of the cash flow. Some facilities have leased a large block of units to a single corporate customer. While this is good business, self-storage space is typically leased on a month-to-month basis. Dependence on a single customer can increase investment risk and the vacancy rate. This increased risk must be considered in the selection of rates.

Market Position of the Subject Property

The market position of the subject property is the analyst's final statement regarding how the subject competes or will be positioned to compete with its competitors. After completing all the steps in the market analysis, the existing or proposed property's position in the submarket should be clear. For example, consider an older, Class C facility located along a freeway in a suburban area. The market position of that property might be described like this:

> The subject property is located in a fast-growing suburban area. The property has average access and good visibility and maintains a better-than-average occupancy level of 93% to 96%. When this property was developed 20 years ago, it was one of two facilities in the submarket. Now six facilities populate the submarket, and the area has grown substantially. The subject property has an inferior location when compared to newer competitors, but offers 24-hour access and storage units at a reasonable rate, which helps to differentiate it from its competitors. The property has an established commercial and residential client base and will likely continue to capture a fair share of residential demand. The short-term expectation is that the property will continue to perform well against the higher-priced competition.

The goal of the market position statement is to show the reader or client how the subject property fits into the competitive submarket. The subject property may have superior or inferior characteristics when compared to the competition. These elements should be described and their relevance to rate and occupancy performance should be discussed.

Conclusion

The goal of self-storage market analysis is to develop an understanding of how market interactions will affect a specific property that is either existing or proposed. These relationships can be viewed from the past, present, or future, but they are always changing and are influenced by a variety of factors. Analysts start by defining the market area and identifying who the competitors are. The performance of existing properties helps to demonstrate demand trends. Potential demand can be quantified using demographic statistics matched with industry ratios such as the total rentable square feet (RSF) per person.

> **Distressed Properties**
> Self storage is a management-sensitive asset that can underperform or outperform market averages, depending on the strength of management. While the major chains tout their management savvy, the best management teams are typically developed by small local groups. If a facility has had management problems, it will likely have a lower-than-average occupancy rate, inconsistent rental rates, and high tenant turnover. For a distressed investment property, the analyst considers the current property status and the time and expenditures required to achieve a stabilized occupancy level.

Within the self-storage industry there tend to be two types of analysts: appraisers and feasibility study experts. Both have their place. Appraisers generally write appraisal reports that are used for financing or other value-related activities. The feasibility professionals concentrate on market and feasibility studies. Some of the feasibility studies tend to be quite detailed and provide good information, but they do not include value analysis. Self-storage appraisals, on the other hand, tend to be rich in value analysis and weak in market analysis.

It is becoming increasingly difficult to uncover good self-storage opportunities in the United States due to the tremendous growth in supply. This is true for all market participants, from the local investor to the national player. Over the next 10 years it will be important to sharpen the analysis of self-storage markets because the business is becoming more mature and risks may be increasing. The amount of capital being invested in individual facilities has been increasing, which sets a higher rate for rents. As a result, participants need a tactical plan for market capture. With good market analysis as a foundation, appraisals can be used to help market participants make better decisions. Valuation techniques and applications are discussed next.

Select Resources

This list represents a selection of established and useful resources for appraisers. Many of these Web sites will have links to additional sources of information.

Publications

Mini-Storage Messenger
  The most comprehensive monthly magazine in the industry
    www.ministoragemessenger.com

Inside Self Storage
  Monthly magazine with good Web site resources
    www.insideselfstorage.com

Self Storage Almanac
  Provides national supply statistics, operating data, customer trends, tenant mix data, and survey of sales data.
    www.ministoragemessenger.com

ISS Factbook
  Resource covering all aspects of the industry
    www.insideselfstorage.com

Building Vendors

Trachte Building Systems (TBS)
  www.trachte.com

Betco Inc.
  www.betcoinc.com

Rib Roof Metal Systems
  www.ribroof.com

Demographics

ESRI Business Information Solutions
  www.esribis.com

Industry Organizations

Self Storage Association (SSA)
  Official association site for self-storage information and education
    www.selfstorage.org

Self Storage Listings

Loopnet
  www.loopnet.com

Argus Self Storage Sales Network
  www.selfstorage.com

Revel and Underwood
  www.revelu.com

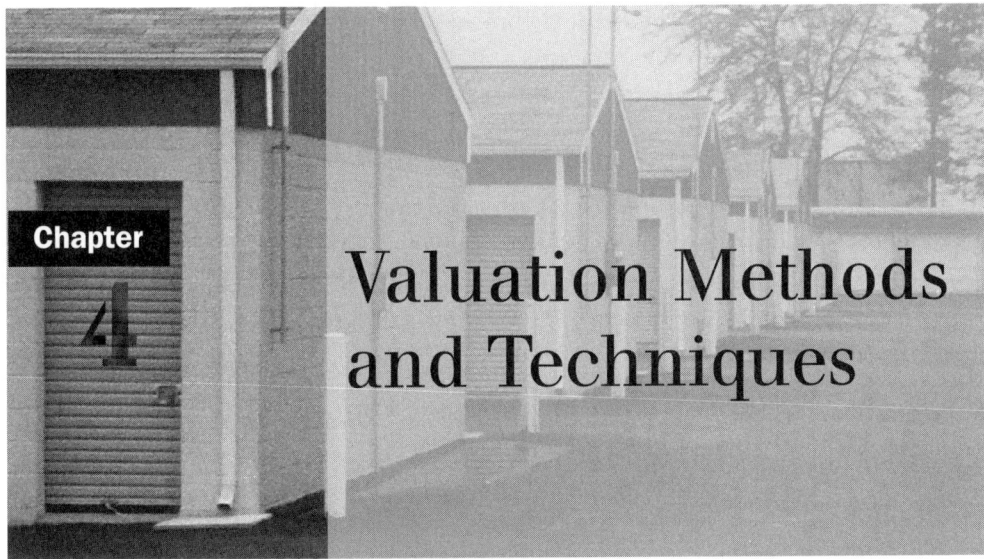

Chapter 4: Valuation Methods and Techniques

This chapter presents general guidelines on how the standard valuation approaches, i.e., sales comparison, cost, and income capitalization, can be used to estimate the value of a self-storage project. Self-storage properties are purchased or developed for the economic benefits of net cash flow and asset appreciation. Most investors are concerned with income performance and the price they pay for a property is based on its income in relation to investment risk. This means that the income capitalization approach is the most relevant approach to use in estimating the value of a self-storage project. The cost approach can be applied to establish a cost basis as a foundation for feasibility analysis. Analysis of sales data in the sales comparison approach can provide insights into the storage investment market that cannot be gained through financial analysis alone.

Sales Comparison Approach

In the sales comparison approach, the physical characteristics of comparable improved sale properties are compared with the subject property to derive an estimate of value for the subject property. This is accomplished by applying units of comparison such as the price per square foot or the price per unit. Units of comparison vary for different property types, and the most reliable unit of comparison for self-storage properties is the price per square foot of gross or net rentable building area. The price per storage unit is applied less frequently because it is not used by market participants and can be misleading since unit mixes can vary. In comparing self-storage facilities, the appraiser should remember to exclude the space occupied by the manager's office and/or apartment unless all the competitive properties have similar features.

Sales data is used in comparing physical property characteristics and an analysis of sales data can reveal good information regarding operating expense ratios and overall capitalization rates. The extraction of overall rates from sales usually provides a good basis for selecting a rate that can be used in the valuation of a specific property.

Strengths and Weaknesses of the Sales Comparison Approach

Appraisers love sales data. A well-researched property sale communicates many things to a professional appraiser. Sales are important because

- They prove that there is an active market for a specific property type.
- They can provide details on operating characteristics such as occupancy rates, expense ratios, and gross revenue.
- They can indicate return relationships and support an overall capitalization rate (R_o), effective gross income multiplier ($EGIM$), or net operating income (NOI) per square foot.
- They can identify industry participants such as lenders, buyers, sellers, and brokers.
- They suggest standard property characteristics such as the typical floor area ratio, size of the office/retail area, site size, and average storage unit size.

An array of good sales indicates many things about a specific property type and market. When sales data is organized on a chart or grid, pricing relationships and the common traits of competitive properties are revealed. However, analyzing sales data to estimate the value of a property has strengths and weaknesses, which are described below.

Quantity and Quality of Data

The usefulness of sales comparison analysis is directly related to the quality and quantity of available sales data. There is an active market for existing self-storage properties. In a large market there may be 10 to 20 sales that can be used as a basis for comparison, whereas in a small market there may only be a few useful sales. The number of recent sales that are available directly influences the strength of this approach.

The quality of sales data is also important and can vary greatly depending on the source of the data. Many participants in the self-storage market are individual investors or mom and pop owners who may not be willing to disclose financial details. The brokers who are involved in self storage can be a very good source of sale information, along with other appraisers and public records. The quality of the sales data will directly impact the strength of the analysis.

Unsupported Adjustments

An analysis that shows too many unsupported adjustments may lose credibility. Appraisals often include huge spreadsheets showing numerous technical adjustments and many lenders feel cheated if they do not see such a chart. In reality the process of adjusting prices is simply an attempt to add or subtract dollars from a transaction price to reflect the inferior or superior components of the comparable property in comparison to the subject property. In the most basic comparison, a sale is judged to be better, worse, or similar to the subject property. At the other end of the spectrum, an appraiser might make a 3.782% adjustment for a paved driveway versus a gravel driveway. The thought process in both cases is the same—quantifying how differences between properties influence their prices.

Problems arise when appraisers develop comparable parameters and adjustments that are not tied to market activity. A property's condition at the time of sale is a major adjustment item and most appraisers and market participants would agree that it influences the property's price. Conversely, an adjustment for two restrooms versus one would probably be too specific to qualify as relevant to a self-storage property. The appraiser must determine which factors influence price in a specific submarket.

For self storage, some of the major considerations are

- Market conditions
- Terms of sale
- Location, including frontage or lack of frontage
- Age, condition, and occupancy at the time of sale
- Quality and size of the improvements
- Excess or surplus land

Each of these elements can have a strong influence on a property's performance and value and is clearly important to investors. Appraisers must remember that all price adjustments should reflect price-influencing differences that are recognized and supported by the market.

Overvaluation

There is a tendency to overvalue self storage and the sales comparison approach can be a useful check on the results from the income capitalization approach. For example, assume the appraiser is estimating the market rent of an existing self-storage facility as part of an appraisal assignment. After all the market research has been completed and the rents have been estimated, a projection of gross potential income is made and the appraiser realizes that the income projection is 25% higher than last year's actual results. This is a common problem because effective rents can vary markedly from published rents. To solve this problem the appraiser checks the market. Comparable sales indicate gross income per square foot and prices per square foot, which may tell the real story of income performance. In this case sales data can help reveal errors that occur in income analysis. Thus, sales comparison analysis can be used to check and balance the income analysis portion of an appraisal.

Market Segmentation

The self-storage market is roughly divided into small, medium, and large segments. The small market includes properties that cost less than $1 million. These are typically mom and pop properties that have less than 25,000 square feet. Participants in small markets are usually small local investors, and this type of property has the least liquidity. The medium-sized market is composed of properties that range in price from $1 million to $3 million. This market is active and will attract local, regional, and some institutional investors. Properties valued at $3 million to $10 million make up the large self-storage market. These highest-quality properties include all the newer multistory and climate-control assets. They attract national and regional private investors and a limited number of institutional investors.

A 25,000-sq.-ft. self-storage facility sale cannot be used as a sale comparable for the valuation of a 5,000-sq.-ft. self-storage property. These storage facilities are simply not comparable properties and sales comparison relies on the comparison of similar properties. Large adjustments can be made to account for vast differences between properties, but it may be preferable to skip the approach altogether or comment on market sales in a narrative fashion. If comparable data is lacking, the practitioner should not force bad comparables into a grid and make massive adjustments to develop some kind of sales analysis.

Good Sales Data

The sales comparison approach depends on good sale data. A sample of a thorough description of a self-storage sale follows.

Sale 1

Name	Storage America
Location	2222 East Green Road
	Columbus, Ohio (SW)
Project grade	B
Project condition at sale	Good–no deferred maintenance
Facility telephone number	1-800-555-1212
Seller	Infinity Partners LLC (local developer)
Buyer	Major Self Storage (regional owner)
Date of sale	January 2003
Sale price	$2,500,000
Recording data	Instrument number 03-222224444
Real property	Fee simple, subject to monthly leases
Conditions of sale	Arm's length
Financing	Conventional mortgage at market terms
Location/land value	Estimated at $300,000 or 12% of sale price
Occupancy at sale	90%
Site description	4.00 acres
Building size/sq. ft. NRA	55,000 sq. ft. (NRA)
Project size/sq. ft. GBA	57,500 sq. ft. (GBA) - includes hallways/office
Climate control	20%
No. of units	450 (in seven buildings)
Type of construction	Metal and concrete block
Year built	1997
Utilities	All available
Zoning	NC, neighborhood commercial
Economic data "as is" in 2002	
GPI	$500,000
Less vacancy	$50,000
EGI	$450,000
Less expenses	$200,000
NOI	$250,000
Expense ratio	44%
OAR	10.0
EGIM	5.56
Price/sq. ft. NRA	$45.45
Source of information	Seller (1-800-666-1111)
Comments	The property reached 90% occupancy 36 months after opening in 1997.
Marketing	The property was sold by Tom Smith, a broker with ABC Realty (1-888-555-1122). He indicated that the facility was listed for three months and that there were two offers during that period. The current sale occurred with the third offer in the fourth month of marketing.

Misleading Sales Data

While past results may be indicative of future trends, this is not always the case in the opportunistic and cyclical world of commercial real estate. Sales that occurred when the market was strong may not reflect a market that is weak. Conversely, sales transacted in a down period may not reflect a market at the beginning of an upward cycle. The self-storage market declined from 1989 to 1993 and improved between 1993 and 1996. It then became very hot from 1996 to 1999 but cooled again in 2000. Brokers who are actively marketing properties are good sources for market condition opinions, which can be converted into market conditions adjustments. These adjustments may also be supported by comparing sales under contract with sales that have already occurred. For the most part, detailed sales data provides good static information that must be considered in light of current market dynamics.

Physical Traits That May Require Adjustment

The building standard for self-storage properties has evolved over the years. While office buildings built in the 1920s are still viable and are rehabilitated in many metropolitan areas around the country, a storage facility that was built in 1955 has probably been converted into another use or fallen into a pile of rubble. Some early storage buildings, and some newer ones, may exhibit low-quality construction components such as wood-pole framing and low-gauge steel construction. Today industry leaders such as Trachte and Betco provide state-of-the-art storage for a variety of applications, including single-story, multistory, and mobile facilities.

Differences between properties can most often be attributed to differences in quality. A wood-frame facility will likely have a higher insurance cost (and built-in obsolescence) when compared to a comparable steel project. An open building that resembles a warehouse may have much lower income per square foot than a building with many smaller units. A specialized building for boat or car storage may also have different income and price characteristics. The interim use of excess land for outdoor storage must be addressed appropriately. Practitioners should not count the outdoor storage income and then add the value of the land as excess land. That would be double counting.

Quality and location are the two largest price-influencers for self-storage properties. Under the quality category, the principle of increasing and decreasing returns comes into play. The highest quality self-storage projects, which have multistory designs, artistic site or facade elements, full climate control, and large retail display areas, may not achieve the rental rates needed to support the operation and compensate for the risk involved. Self storage is still just storage, and in most markets there are price limits created by competitive alternatives. While quality is an important price-influencer, the contribution of quality must be viewed as it relates to income performance.

Adjustment Using Net Operating Incomes

Table 4.1 summarizes sales data on a subject property and three comparable properties that sold on the same day, just before the appraisal date.

Table 4.1

	Subject Property	Sale 1	Sale 2	Sale 3
Sale price	—	$2,000,000	$1,900,000	$2,200,000
NOI	$210,000	$200,000	$190,000	$220,000
Size/sq. ft. NRA	35,000	35,000	35,000	35,000
NOI/sq. ft.	$6.00	$5.71	$5.43	$6.29
Price/sq. ft.	—	$57.14	$54.29	$62.86

The prices of the sales range from $54.29 to $62.86 per square foot. The only difference between the sales is the performance indicated by the net income. An adjustment based on the net operating income is a reasonable way to account for differences between the properties. The differences between the net operating incomes of comparable stabilized properties provide a strong basis for adjustment. The adjustment process is shown in Table 4.2

Table 4.2

	Subject Property	Sale 1	Sale 2	Sale 3
Price/sq. ft.	—	$57.14	$54.29	$62.86
NOI/sq. ft.	$6.00	$5.71	$5.43	$6.29
Subject property NOI/sq. ft.	$6.00	$6.00	$6.00	$6.00
Adjustment	—	+5%	+10.5%	−5%
Adj. price/sq. ft.	—	$60.00	$60.00	$60.00

After adjustment, the sales show an adjusted price per square foot of approximately $60. Since the facility has 35,000 square feet, its value is estimated to be $2,100,000. In this example, an *NOI* adjustment process is applied instead of quantifying adjustments for individual property components. This can only be accomplished when net operating income data is available for each sale property.

The only shortfall of this method is that the comparable properties must be very similar to the subject. The technique will not produce reliable results if the subject and comparables have different income streams. In this case, there is a need for a compensating adjustment to the sales. For example, a facility with climate-controlled space should not be compared to one without climate-controlled space. Similarly, a facility with outside storage is not comparable to a facility without outside storage. Adjustments must be made for differences in the properties' revenue sources.

The use of sales data provides strong support for valuation and analysis in most situations. Problems occur when there is a limited number of sales, when sales are dated, and when sales do not truly reflect comparable properties. When a substantial amount of quality data is available, the status of the market is usually self-evident and little additional analysis is needed. Good sales analysis in a valuation is a good check on the results of income analysis and enhances the quality of the value opinion. The inclusion of sales analysis in self-storage valuation is important. Even if there are few sales to analyze, the sales market should be discussed. This discussion may include information from broker or investor interviews, data on regional sales trends, and targeted rates of return.

Cost Approach

Over the years the cost to develop self-storage projects has increased, largely because facilities are being built on superior sites and building code requirements are stricter. Today an assessment of the financial viability of a project is crucial. For the most part, the self-storage market has been able to absorb the increased costs of development by charging higher rents for the convenience and quality of newer facilities. As a general rule, the cost to develop a Class C self-storage project, including the land and all soft and hard costs, should range from $45 to $70 per square foot. A facility in a rural location may cost less and a higher-quality, multistory facility may cost more. The cost of land for self-storage facilities varies widely depending on whether they are located in rural, suburban, or urban areas.

Cost and market value are closely related when properties are new, so the value estimate derived using the cost approach is most persuasive for new or relatively new self-storage facilities. The cost approach can be applied to older properties given adequate data to measure depreciation. The cost approach is also useful in calculating adjustments for differences in the physical characteristics of comparable properties in the sales comparison approach. If, for example, an appraiser must adjust a comparable sale price for an inadequate HVAC system, the cost to cure the deficiency can be used as a basis for this adjustment in the sales comparison approach.

The estimate of value developed by the cost approach is often thought of as an upper limit of value. An investor will not pay $4 million to acquire an existing self-storage facility if the cost to develop a comparable facility from the ground up is only $3 million. Thus, the cost of a proposed property is useful for determining financial feasibility. To use a simplified example, assume a proposed self-storage development has a cost basis of $3 million and an overall capitalization rate of 10% is applicable at stabilization. The following net income would be needed to satisfy the yield requirement.

$$\begin{array}{r}3{,}000{,}000\\ \times\quad 0.10\\ \hline \$\,300{,}000\end{array}$$

The project must produce $300,000 of net operating income at a stabilized occupancy and operating level to be considered financially feasible. (A detailed cost breakdown for feasibility analysis will be illustrated in Chapter 5.)

The first step in the cost approach is to estimate the value of the site as though vacant. Then the hard and soft costs of the project are estimated and an amount is added for entrepreneurial incentive. (For existing properties, the appraiser can determine the actual entrepreneurial profit earned rather than the reward anticipated for the entrepreneur's investment of time and expertise.) Any depreciation in the subject property is then identified and deducted from the total cost of the improvements. Finally, the resulting figure is added to the land value to provide an indication of value for the subject property.

Depreciation

Depreciation comes in three forms:

1. Physical deterioration—wear and tear from regular use and the impact of the elements.
2. Functional obsolescence—a flaw in the structure, materials, or design that diminishes the function, utility, and value of the improvement.
3. External obsolescence—a temporary or permanent impairment of the utility or salability of an improvement or property due to negative influences outside the property.[1]

Physical deterioration is the easiest form of depreciation to identify and assess. The appraiser can identify items of deferred maintenance or the deterioration of short- and long-lived items during physical inspection of the subject property and estimate the cost to cure these items. Items of physical deterioration commonly found in self-storage facilities include

- Faded building paint
- Deteriorated asphalt
- Deteriorated concrete
- Aging fencing
- Outdated office interior
- Outdated HVAC system

---

1. Appraisal Institute, *The Appraisal of Real Estate*, 12th ed. (Chicago: Appraisal Institute, 2001).

Functional obsolescence is generally the most difficult form of depreciation to estimate. Knowledge of the market is needed to determine which characteristics of an older property do not meet current market expectations and which are considered overimprovements. The most common causes of functional obsolescence in self-storage properties include

- Poor unit layout. Even new self-storage facilities can suffer from functional obsolescence if the space is poorly designed.
- Crowded placement of buildings. There should be adequate space for truck loading and turning.
- Buildings positioned too deep on a site. Units far from the office are perceived to be less secure and convenient.
- Vertical space in a nonvertical market. The latest trend is to build multistory buildings, but upper-floor units may not be well accepted in some markets.

Exernal obsolescence is often incurable and can affect both the land and the improvements. Market analysis will generally reveal if there is an imbalance in the market that affects the value of the subject property, such as an oversupply of similar properties. Market-related external obsolescence may decrease over time as supply and demand in the market move toward equilibrium. A value loss due to an undesirable location must be accounted for in the estimation of external obsolescence and is likely to be permanent.

Strengths and Weaknesses of the Cost Approach

For a Proposed Project

The budgeted costs for a proposed self-storage project provide a basis for testing its feasibility. In the case of a proposed project, the cost approach is useful for analyzing land values and estimating the cost breakdown of a new facility. Assessing the relationship between cost and value can be informative for market participants and enhance their decision making.

For an Existing Project

There is no doubt that the cost new to replace a project is important information for any appraiser. The replacement cost of a project suggests the cost of entry into the market and is relevant when an investor is considering whether to buy or build a facility. The problem arises when the cost analysis becomes a tool for valuing an existing project. Investors simply do not use depreciated cost as a basis for making purchasing decisions so this approach is not directly tied to the market.

Conclusion

In the valuation of existing self-storage properties, the cost approach is generally not relevant for several reasons:

1. The estimates of value generated by the sales comparison and income capitalization approaches are often well-supported and persuasive, while the depreciation estimates needed to apply the cost approach are often difficult to support.
2. Market participants including owners, investors, developers, and brokers do not rely on depreciated cost estimates as a basis for estimating prices.
3. The cost to replace an existing property has little relevance to the "as is" value of the property.

Income Capitalization Approach and Operating Expense Analysis

In analyzing the financial operations of an existing or proposed self-storage project, the appraiser first analyzes the property's income potential. Most income is derived from renting storage units of various sizes to users on a monthly basis. The estimation of potential gross income (*PGI*) is based on the steps completed in market analysis, which include the development of market rental rates for each type of unit in the unit mix. The potential gross income is the maximum amount of income that could be achieved at full occupancy and market rental rates. Projecting lease-up rates and effective rent are two of the most important aspects of an accurate forecast.

Rental Income

A typical self-storage project generates income from a variety of sources, including the rental of individual storage units and outdoor storage. Current or projected rent may be used but the anticipated future income is the benchmark for valuation and feasibility. Most investors are interested in the income that will be generated by a property operation. A property's earning history is important, but the future earnings form the basis for valuation.

Other Income

A self-storage project can generate income from other revenue sources as well, including retail sales, late fees, insufficient funds fees, administrative fees, forfeited security deposits, and vending machines. Retail sales revenue is generated by the sale of mov-

> "Self-storage lenders have become increasingly sophisticated in their underwriting, aiding the entire industry by demanding the solid fundamentals necessary for success."
> - Broker Michael Haugh, CCIM

> If the actual effective income from an existing project is much less than the income projection, then the practitioner probably has not accounted for rent concessions, which may include free rent and discounts.

ing-related supplies such as boxes, locks, tape, and wrapping materials. Some revenue, such as truck rental income, is not real estate-based and should be considered as business revenue.

Other income generally ranges from 3% to 10% of effective gross rental income and 4% to 6% of effective gross income. The amount and durability of this income is heavily dependent on the location and configuration of each facility. A facility with a large retail sales area or a truck rental operation can generate a higher-than-average stream of other income. A facility with no retail sales operation will not generate any retail sales revenue, but it will likely generate revenue through late fees and other fees.

Business Components

Many self-storage properties are sold with inventory or with operations such as a truck rental business. The truck rental business is a separate entity that is not real estate-dependent and its value should be deducted from the sale price. All expenses and income that are attributable to such an operation must be excluded from the real estate valuation. A truck rental operation is equipment-dependent, with licenses and other agreements that are not related to the real estate.

The sale of packing and storage supplies, on the other hand, generates net income and can be considered part of the overall real estate operation. If the sale of packing and storage supplies is more substantial than usual and generates a large percentage of bottom-line income, the risk of the self-storage investment would increase. The appraiser should deal with such an aberration carefully and make sure that retail sales income is not considered the same as rental income. If the retail space is leased to a third-party operator, that lease income must be considered as a separate line item and the lease value must be carefully examined.

Vacancy and Collection Loss

The deduction for vacancy and collection loss is an annualized figure that reflects specific submarket trends. The deduction shown in the stabilized operating statement should reflect market expectations–i.e., if properties in the submarket consistently show an 85% occupancy rate, then the stabilized occupancy rate for the subject property would likely be 85%.

Expense Analysis

There is no established standard of accounts for self-storage projects, but a typical operating statement for an existing self-storage project is illustrated in Figure 4.1.

Multipliers and *NOI* per Square Foot Analysis

The income and expense data provided by comparable sales can be used to develop multipliers that can be applied in valuing a property by the income capitalization approach. Income and expense information for a subject property and comparable improved sales is summarized in Table 4.3.

Figure 4.1 Sample Operating Statement

Any Self Storage
Net rentable area (NRA) = 37,000 sq. ft.

Income	Stabilized 2004	Dollars Per Sq. Ft. of NRA	% of EGI
Gross potential rental income (GPI)—stabilized	$350,000	$9.46	
Less: vacancy and collection loss @ 7%	$24,500	0.66	
Effective gross rental income (EGI)	$325,500	$8.80	
Other income @ 4%:	$13,020	0.35	
Total effective gross income (EGI)	$338,520	$9.15	100%
Expenses			
Advertising	$8,000	$0.22	2%
Administrative	9,000	0.24	3%
Staff salaries & benefits	38,000	1.03	11%
Professional fees	3,000	0.08	1%
Management fee @ 5% of EGI	16,926	0.46	5%
Utilities (partial climate control)	10,000	0.27	3%
Repairs and maintenance	6,000	0.16	2%
Insurance	4,000	0.11	1%
Real estate taxes	30,000	0.81	9%
Reserves	0	0.00	0%
Total expenses	$124,926	$3.38	37%
Net operating income	$213,594	$5.77	
Expense ratio	37%		

Table 4.3 Sample Income and Expenses

	Subject Property	Sale 1	Sale 2	Sale 3	Sale 4
Sale price	—	$1,700,000	$1,200,000	$1,450,000	$1,900,000
Effective gross income	$215,000	$250,000	$170,000	$200,000	$275,000
Expenses	$68,600	$88,500	$50,000	$58,625	$85,000
Expense ratio	32%	35%	29%	29%	31%
NOI	$146,400	$161,500	$120,000	$141,375	$190,000
OAR (R_o)	—	9.5%	10.0%	9.8%	10.0%
EGIM	—	6.8	7.1	7.3	6.9

The overall capitalization rate is calculated by dividing the net operating income of a property by its total sale price. The effective gross income multiplier (*EGIM*) is developed by dividing a property's sale price by the effective gross income. Both investment parameters can be used to derive an estimate of value for an income-producing property.

For example, the net operating income projected for the subject property is $146,400. The overall capitalization rates indicated by the comparable improved sales range from 9.5% to 10%. These rates would provide the following value indications:

Subject Property NOI		EGIM		Value
$146,400	÷	0.095	=	$1,541,053
$146,400	÷	0.098	=	$1,493,878
$146,400	÷	0.100	=	$1,464,000

The value indications provided by this direct capitalization method can be supported by applying the *EGIM*s of the comparable properties to the subject's projected effective gross income. The subject's projected stabilized effective gross income is $215,000 and the comparables' *EGIM*s range from 6.8 to 7.3. The value indications are calculated below.

Subject Property NOI		EGIM		Value
$215,000	×	6.8	=	$1,462,000
$215,000	×	6.9	=	$1,483,500
$215,000	×	7.1	=	$1,526,500
$215,000	×	7.3	=	$1,569,500

The *EGIM* analysis results in a value range of $1,462,000 to $1,569,500 for the subject, which is supported by the direct capitalization method. The *EGIM* applicable to the subject can be further tested using the following formula:

$$\frac{1 - \text{expense ratio}}{R_o} = \frac{1 - 36\%}{9.5\%} = \frac{0.64}{0.095} = 6.74$$

The calculation indicates that the subject's expense ratio is too high because the R_o is at the low end of the sale comparables' range.

Common Appraisal Mistakes

Five flaws are commonly found in self-storage appraisals and feasibility studies.

1. Aggressive income forecasts
2. Unfounded absorption assumptions
3. Poor market surveys

4. Low expense ratios
5. Poor R_o development

Aggressive Income Forecasts

Practitioners should be careful not to overestimate income; income estimates must be grounded in actual performance. If the earning history of an existing self-storage property indicates $300,000 in net operating income, the income is probably not going to increase substantially even though this may be suggested by the analysis of market rental rates. Effective rental rates in this market segment are volatile and affected by special discounts and seasonal fluctuations.

Unfounded Absorption Assumptions

The lease-up projection for a new property must be tied to observed and probable market activity. The use of industry rules of thumb, developer-created pro forma statements, and single-asset comparisons can lead to unfounded absorption assumptions. Invariably, the result is an overly optimistic projection.

Poor Market Surveys

Surveying any self-storage market involves legwork and telephone calls. Taking shortcuts, such as using only a few rent comparables or not completing interviews, will result in a weaker analysis.

Low Expense Ratios

A self-storage project is a management-intensive asset and many projects' operating expenses for real estate taxes, insurance, utilities, and labor costs increase. Expense ratios equal to 30% to 35% of effective gross stabilized income are common. An expense analysis that does not account for management and labor costs will likely result in a lower-than-average expense projection.

Poor R_o Development

In this market, the overall capitalization rate (R_o), or cap rate, indicates pricing and yield performance. Most market participants freely discuss R_o targets for acquisitions and development. Such discussions are common in the self-storage industry and an appraiser can learn a great deal by listening to brokers and investors who are active market participants.

Conclusion

Real estate professionals always strive to do better. An appraiser can conduct one more interview or find one better comparable to further inform and refine the analysis. Appraisal reports are prepared to give clients a well-founded value opinion and market information they can use to make decisions. The pressure to provide opinions to meet a deadline is a constant in the appraiser's world, but this pressure must never limit the analysis undertaken by appraisers or adversely affect the services they provide.

The three approaches to value are used together because each has strengths and can be used as a check and balance against the others. The sales comparison approach proves that investor demand exists and establishes unit prices that reflect market activity. The income approach translates actual rental activity into a projection of investment results and the value of the income is measured against market alternatives. In both approaches actual market activity is analyzed and presented to support an opinion of value. These valuation methods are dynamic because they are tied to shifting market forces that are influenced by innumerable variables. The cost approach is more static and much less relevant in the analysis of existing properties.

Chapter 5

Case Study: Proposed Falls River Self Storage

This case study shows how the principles that have been discussed can be applied to an actual appraisal consulting assignment. The client, Falls River Real Estate Development and Management, has approached the appraiser for an objective opinion of the financial feasibility of the proposed Falls River Self Storage facility. The appraiser realizes that in addition to a market study of competitive supply and demand, he will need to evaluate the highest and best use of the site as vacant and as improved and to analyze the potential income and operating expenses of the proposed property.

The appraiser first collects data on the property and market and prepares a description of the subject site, the proposed improvements, and the market area. Then a market study is undertaken to determine the market acceptance of the proposed property. In this case study, two situations will be presented—one in which the development is feasible and one in which it is not—to illustrate the difference. After highest and best use analysis, the income capitalization approach will be applied to estimate the value of the property upon completion of construction and upon stabilized occupancy. Those value estimates will be compared with the budgeted costs of the proposed improvements to reach a conclusion on the project's financial feasibility.

Property and Market Data

The basic characteristics of the proposed property are described below.

Property Characteristics

Name	Falls River Self Storage
Location	9600 Eagle River Road
	Indianapolis, Indiana
Site size	4.50 acres; 196,020 sq. ft. ±
Land to building ratio	2.82:1
Excess/surplus land	None
Proposed gross building area	69,500 sq. ft.
Proposed net rentable area	61,400 sq. ft.
Area breakdown	41,400 sq. ft. regular storage space
	20,000 sq. ft. climate-controlled storage space
	6,000 sq. ft. interior hallways
	2,100 sq. ft. two-story office/apartment
	69,500 sq. ft.
No. of storage units	515
Average unit size	119 sq. ft.

The proposed net rentable area is the area that is dedicated to self-storage space. The gross building area includes common area space such as hallways, the office, and the on-site manager's apartment. The proposed site plan for the facility is shown in Figure 5.1.

Regional Influences

The area trends are generally positive and the northeast side is an affluent and growing suburban region. Information on the metropolitan area in which the subject is located is shown in Table 5.1.

Table 5.1 Metropolitan Area Analysis

Factor	Description	Quantification
Metropolitan area	Indianapolis	Ranked 21 in size in the United States
Metropolitan employment base	Diversified	—
Population	Growing	1% per year
Unemployment	Low	Under 3%
Market access	Good	—
Northeast Side of Metropolitan Area		
Population	High growth	5% per year
Household income	High	$45,000 +
Character of area	Suburban	80% developed

Figure 5.1 Site Plan

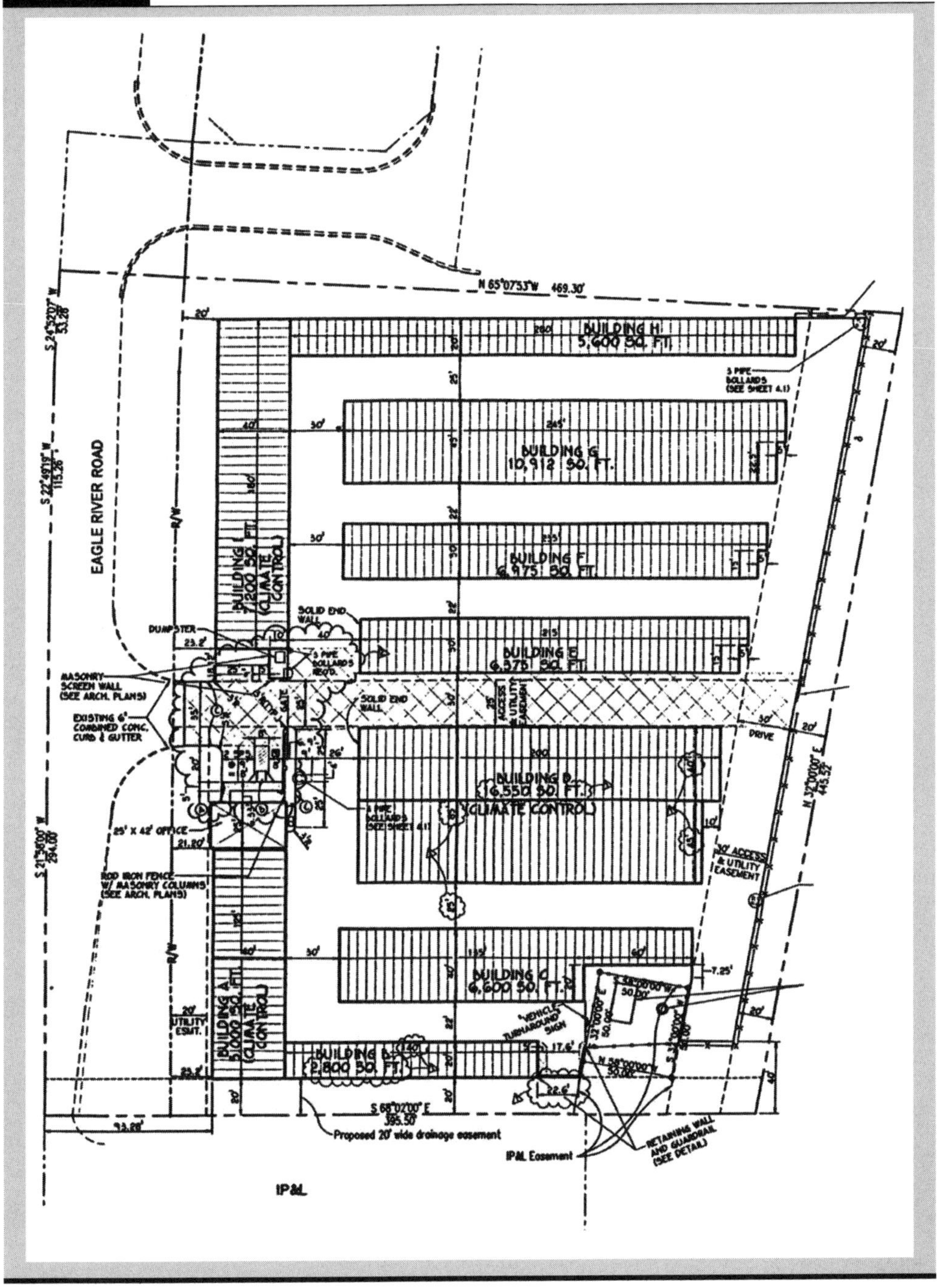

Case Study: Proposed Falls River Self Storage

> The depth and focus of the area review, which is macro in nature, depends on the type of assignment or analysis. Many appraisals contain laborious discussions of area economic facts and trends, which may be appropriate or may be exhausting. In today's information-rich environment, it is easy to obtain economic data for any location in the country. The appraiser's task is to apply these facts and trends to the subject property. Area trends set the tone for more specific submarket analysis that follows.

Neighborhood Characteristics

The subject property is located near the intersection of Eagle River Road and 79th Street on the northeast side of Indianapolis. There are three shopping centers at this intersection, including a grocery store-anchored neighborhood center known as Falls Crossing and three small strip centers. Outparcels of the Falls Crossing retail center have been developed with a bank branch, an oil lube facility, and a fast-food restaurant. This center also includes the subject property, which is sandwiched between the shopping center and an adjacent electrical substation. This intersection can be described as a neighborhood retail district that has been developed over the past 10 years and serves the needs of the local population.

Outside this small retail district, the area predominantly comprises new and existing residential subdivisions. The Deer Run subdivision, located across the street from the subject site, is approximately 80% developed, with homes ranging in price from $400,000 to $800,000. The immediate neighborhood has a variety of housing consisting mostly of detached single-family developments, with some townhomes and apartments.

The neighborhood is growing, and a moderate volume of commuter traffic moves through the area on a daily basis. The subject property is well positioned to capitalize on the storage needs of an affluent and growing residential population. A neighborhood map is shown in Figure 5.2.

Figure 5.2 Neighborhood Map

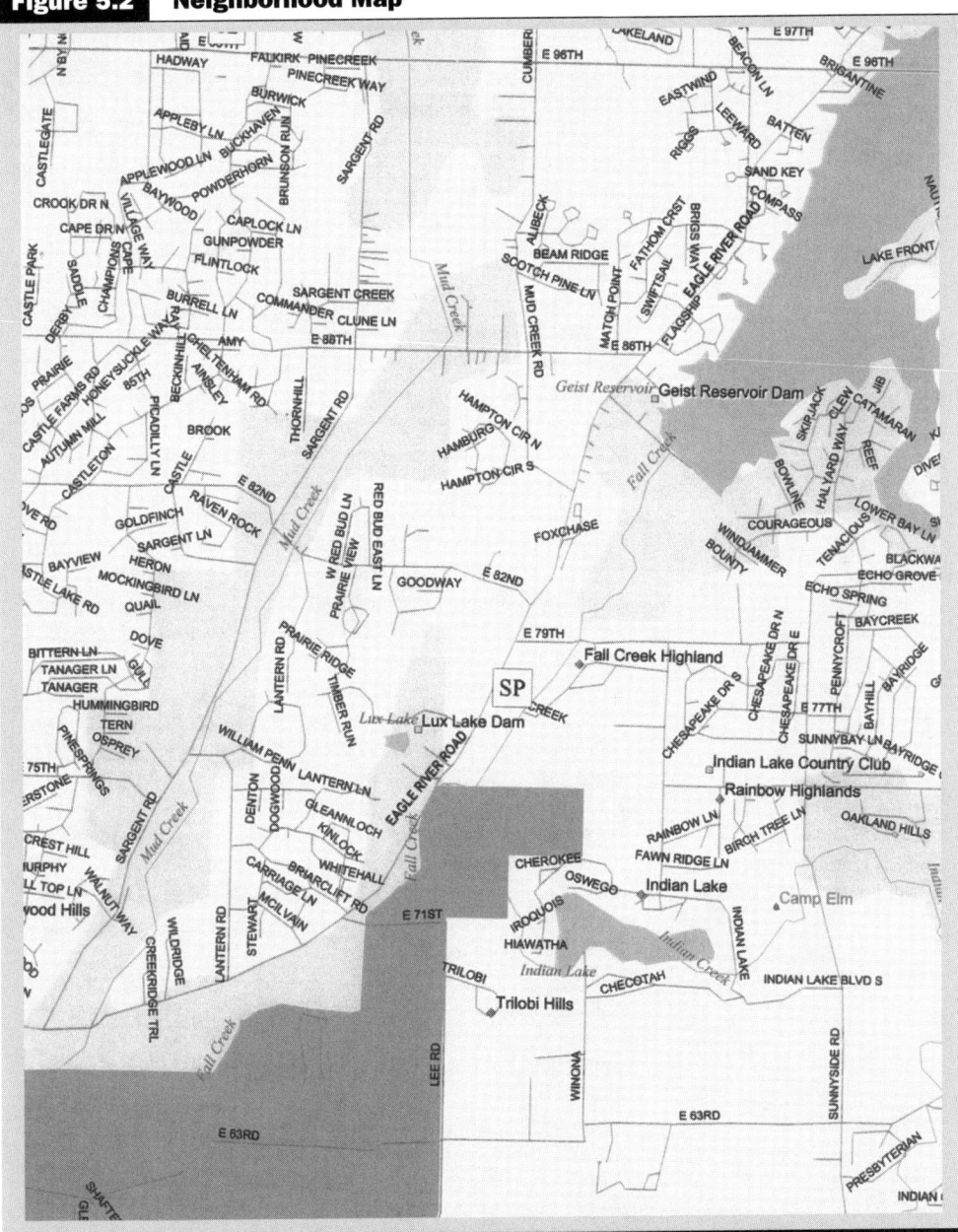

* SP = subject property

Case Study: Proposed Falls River Self Storage

Site Description, Zoning, and Assessment

Following is a brief description of the subject site.

Size	4.50 acres; 196,020 sq. ft. ±
Topography/shape	The site is rectangular, at road grade, and level throughout. The overall shape and topography of the subject site are conducive to development.
Ingress/egress	The property has one curb cut providing direct access to Eagle River Road and additional access from shared entrance drives within the shopping center. The site has approximately 462 feet of frontage along Eagle River Road and is clearly visible from this thoroughfare. Both access and visibility are adequate.
Street improvements	Eagle River Road is a two-lane, asphalt-paved arterial road with a painted center turn lane extending along the frontage of Falls Crossing shopping center.
Utilities	Municipal water and sewer are provided by the city. All other utilities are available to the site.
Easements	It is assumed that the property is subject to standard utility easements, which do not necessarily hinder site utility. No other easements were noted.
Flood zone	According to Flood Insurance Rate Map 180159-0020, effective June 1988, the subject is located in an area that experiences minimal flooding.
Soil and subsoil	No soil or subsoil reports were made available to the appraiser. It is assumed that no environmental hazards that would impact the subject property's value exist.
Wetlands	According to the plat and site plan provided for this analysis, the subject site does not contain wetlands. The valuation is based on the assumption that there are no wetlands located on the subject site.
Nuisances and hazards	The subject property is adjacent to an electrical substation, but the proximity of the substation does not adversely impact the subject property.
Zoning	The site is zoned C-3, commercial district, by the City of Indianapolis. The C-3 district allows for a wide variety of general commercial uses, including self storage. The proposed development plan has been approved by local planning authorities.
Assessment	The projected annual real estate taxes, after development, are estimated to be $74,000, or $1.06 per square foot, based on a gross building area of 69,500 square feet. The projected taxes are comparable to current taxes for self-storage projects of similar quality in the region.

Description of the Proposed Improvements

The following description is based on a review of the architectural plans and specifications for the proposed improvements.

Figure 5.3 shows details of the proposed improvements.

Structure class	Class B mini-warehouse
Proposed area	2,100 sq. ft. office/apartment—two stories
	6,000 sq. ft. interior space—hallways
	<u>61,400</u> sq. ft. storage net rentable area (NRA)
	69,500 sq. ft.
Climate-controlled area	20,000 sq. ft. (33% of NRA)
Regular storage	41,400 sq. ft. (67% of NRA)
No. of units	515
Age	Proposed
Foundation	4-in. reinforced concrete slab
Frame/exterior walls	Masonry with smooth-faced concrete block walls
Office/apartment	A 1,050-sq.-ft. office will be located on the first floor. The office floor plan includes a customer reception area, a small restroom, and a garage storage area. The manager's apartment will be located on the second floor, directly above the office, and will also contain 1,050 square feet. The apartment floor plan includes a small den, a kitchen, a laundry room, two bedrooms, and one full bath.
Storage buildings	There will be nine storage buildings. Seven buildings will be positioned perpendicular to Eagle River Road, and two buildings will be positioned parallel to Eagle River Road. The development plan indicates that the subject property will be enclosed to enhance the property's curb appeal.
	Each unit will have a metal roll-up door and interior incandescent lighting. The project will have a central security system. The climate-controlled buildings have a central entry door to an interior hallway. The buildings have an eave height of 8.5 feet.
Roof	Each storage building will have a gently sloped roof covered with prefabricated metal panels.
HVAC systems	The office/apartment building will have a forced-air heating and cooling system. The climate-controlled storage buildings will have forced-air gas heating and air-conditioning units per their specifications.
Fire	No sprinklers
Security	Central office security system
Electricity	1,200 amp, 120/240 volt service
Insulation	None
Site improvements	There will be four asphalt-paved parking spaces at the rental office and asphalt paving between the storage buildings. The area between the buildings will be 22 to 25 feet wide to allow for an adequate loading area and turning radius. The perimeter of the property will be secured with a chain-link fence. Access to the site will be controlled by a security gate at the main entrance. The site will be attractively landscaped.
Functional utility	The project will have a functional layout, and the positioning of the buildings will add to its overall appeal. The materials used are appropriate and will be utilized to maximize the property's market appeal.

Figure 5.3 Proposed Improvements

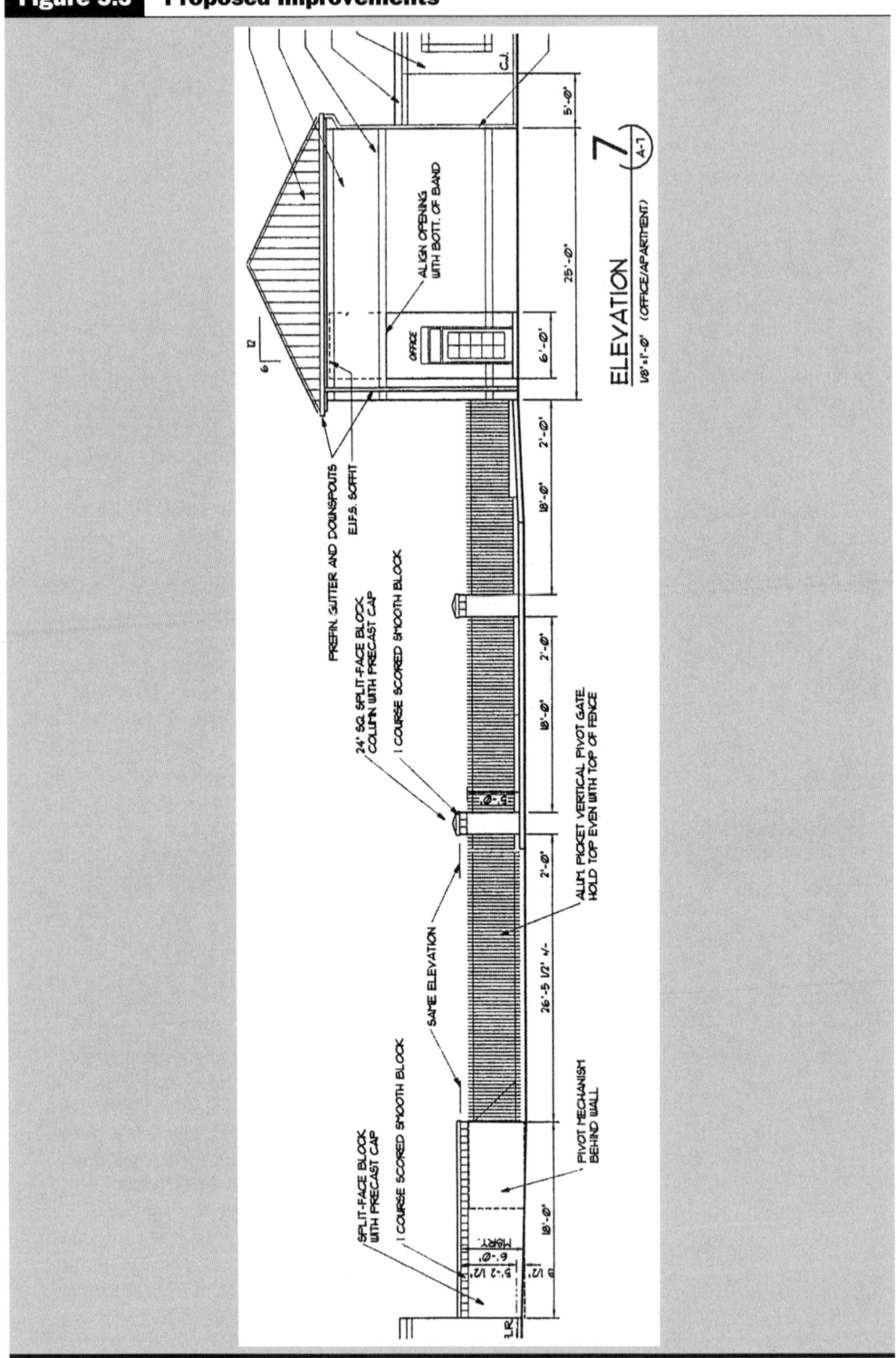

Market Analysis

Like any property, the performance of a self-storage project is influenced by the balance between supply and demand in the market. This section discusses factors that would support the feasibility of the proposed development as well as factors that may indicate that the proposed development is not feasible. Following is a brief analysis of the local market.

Self-Storage Market Trends

The sophistication and location of self-storage facilities have evolved over the past 10 years. For many years, self-storage facilities were located along freeway frontage roads or in industrial parks. New facilities are more commonly developed in retail districts or along heavily traveled commercial corridors. The newest self-storage developments have sections devoted to climate-controlled storage, an on-site apartment and office, and state-of-the-art security systems. The subject property will have all these features.

As previously noted, many companies provide turnkey operations to investors, allowing inexperienced operators to enter the market easily. The proliferation of turnkey operations, the availability and low cost of capital, and the booming economy resulted in a proliferation of new storage development between 1996 and 2001. Although the demand for storage remains strong, the increased level of supply has resulted in increased vacancy in many submarkets, including the subject market in northeast suburban Indianapolis.

Definition of the Market Area

A typical storage development competes within a narrowly defined market area. A market area is sometimes defined as a circle around the subject property. More often, market areas exhibit an irregular pattern, depending on the asset type and linkages to the property. The primary competitive market area for a self-storage facility is usually the three- to five-mile area surrounding the facility. In light of the density of the surrounding population base, the primary market area for the subject property is within a three-mile radius.

Existing Supply

Indianapolis had a total of 187 self-storage facilities in 2002 (up from 170 the previous year) containing a total of 7,130,871 square feet. These facilities served a population of 1,625,201, which indicates that there were 4.39 rentable square feet (RSF) of storage space per person in the Indianapolis market.

In 1996 the existing storage space in the Indianapolis market equated to 2.57 RSF per person, which indicates a significant increase in storage space construction over the six years. In fact, the increase in storage supply has exceeded the rate of population growth in this market. While this growth rate is significant, it is not unusual for Midwestern cities, as is evidenced by the supply trends for four cities between 1996 and 2001 (see Table 5.2). The increasing supply of storage space exceeded the rate of population growth in many Midwestern cities between 1996 and 2001, resulting in increases in the amount of rentable square feet of storage space per person.

To analyze the existing supply of storage space in the subject's defined market area, competing facilities in the north and northeast submarkets were identified and surveyed. A map of the competing facilities is provided in Figure 5.4; a supply survey (Table 5.3) and a summary of the survey results follow.

Table 5.2 Self-Storage Supply 1996 and 2001

City	1996 RSF per Person	2001 RSF per Person	% Change
Indianapolis, IN	2.57	4.39	+71
Columbus, OH	2.67	4.34	+63
St. Louis, MO	2.58	3.63	+41
Cincinnati, OH	2.34	3.73	+59

Based on information from *Self Storage Almanac 2002*.

Figure 5.4 Competing Facilities

SP = subject property

Table 5.3 Supply Survey

Rent Comparables	1		2		3		4		5		6	
	Stuff It Storage		Store It Storage		Safe Storage		Simple Storage		Secure It Storage		Save It Storage	
	900 Allison Road		7100 Milo Road		9200 Corporate Drive		1000 East 16th Street		7000 East 86th Street		370 Breaker Drive	
	Fishers (NE)		Indianapolis (NE)		Indianapolis (NE)		Indianapolis (NE)		Indianapolis (NE)		Indianapolis (N)	
Contact	Mike		Jack		Sarah		Jake		Matt		Tom	
Phone number	567-9090		567-8090		567-0987		567-3245		567-7000		567-2100	
No. of buildings	20		7		10		14		11		5	
No. of units	654		281		377		362		324		650	
Year built	1987 and 1995		1985		1988		1990		1964		1996	
Residential	60%		70%		75%		70%		95%		60%	
Commercial	40%		30%		25%		30%		5%		40%	

	January 1997	January 2001	January 1997	January 2001	January 1997	January 2001	January 1997	January 2001	January 1997	January 2001	January 1997	January 2001
Occupancy	63%	72%	70%	76%	85%	73%	85%	83%	90%	80%	65%	87%
Rent increase/decrease	0%		0%		0%		0%		0%		0%	
Construction	Frame/brick		Frame/block		Block		Metal		Metal/block		Brick	
Building area (sq. ft. NRA)	87,491		30,575		48,480		25,410		38,300		70,240	
Avg. unit size (sq. ft.)	134		109		129		70		118		108	
Other	On-site apt./office		On-site apt./office		On-site apt./office		On-site office		On-site office		On-site apt./office	
Comment											Two-story section	

Unit Size (sq. ft.)	Climate	Regular	Climate	Regular	Climate	Regular	Climate	Regular	Climate	Regular	Climate	Regular
5 × 5	$39	$33	—	$39	—	$35	—	$35	—	$45	—	$39
5 × 10	61	45	—	56	—	43	—	45	—	—	—	56
5 × 15	93	63	—	81	—	—	—	—	—	—	—	72
5 × 20	—	—	—	—	—	—	—	—	—	—	—	—
10 × 10	117	71	—	94	—	71	—	65	—	60	—	83
10 × 15	—	89	—	115	—	89	—	75	—	80	—	114
10 × 20	197	109	—	149	—	113	—	80	—	105	—	135
10 × 25	229	115	—	179	—	165	—	—	—	—	—	—
10 × 30	—	125	—	189	—	—	—	—	—	—	—	—
10 × 40	—	229	—	279	—	—	—	110	—	—	—	—
10 × 50	—	—	—	—	—	—	—	—	—	—	—	—
15 × 20	—	—	—	—	—	—	—	—	—	—	—	—
15 × 25	—	183	—	—	—	—	—	—	—	—	—	—
15 × 40	—	159	—	—	—	—	—	—	—	—	—	—
20 × 15	—	—	—	—	—	—	—	—	—	—	—	—
20 × 20	—	—	—	—	—	—	—	—	—	—	—	—
20 × 25	—	199	—	—	—	—	—	—	—	—	—	—
20 × 30	—	—	—	—	—	—	—	—	—	—	—	—
20 × 40	—	—	—	—	—	—	—	—	—	—	—	—
30 × 30	—	399	—	—	—	—	—	—	—	—	—	—

Table 5.3 Suppply Survey (continued)

Rent Comparables	7 The Storage Place 133 Park Drive Fishers (NE)			8 A Storage Place 2345 Main Street Indianapolis(N)			9 Safer Self Storage 1265 Careful Drive Fishers (NE)			10 State Storage 6800 State Street Fishers (NE)			11 More Secure Self Storage 1212 Deer Run Road Indianapolis (NE)			12 Store Stuff Storage 8800 Main Drive Fishers (NE)		
Contact	Dave			Jan			Ron			Debbie			Bev			Steve		
Phone number	567-4444			567-5656			567-0234			567-3211			567-0945			567-1100		
No. of buildings	8			3			9			4			5			5		
No. of units	400			470			540			143			447			418		
Year built	1995–1996			1996			1997			1984/1996			1998			1998		
Residential	75%			80%			65%			50%			70%			70%		
Commercial	25%			20%			35%			50%			30%			30%		
	January 1997	January 2001		January 1997	January 2001		January 1997	January 2001		January 1997	January 2001		January 1997	January 2001		January 1997	January 2001	
Occupancy	70%	80%		75%	92%		30%	80%		72%	94%		N/A	81%		N/A	77%	
Rent increase/decrease	0%			0%			0%			0%			0%			0%		
Construction	Metal/brick			Concrete			Block			Metal/brick			Metal/block			Brick		
Building area (sq. ft. NRA)	40,000			65,000			69,900			17,600			52,000			60,000		
Avg. unit size (sq. ft.)	100			138			129			123			116			144		
Other	On-site office			On-site apt./office			On-site apt./office			On-site office			On-site apt./office			On-site office		
Comment																		
Unit Size (sq. ft.)	Climate	Regular		Climate	Regular		Climate	Regular		Climate	Regular		Climate	Regular		Climate	Regular	
5 × 5	$45	$35		$77	$35		$50	$40		—	—		$46	$35		$52	$39	
5 × 10	44	40		77	67		90	50		—	45		75	50		66	49	
5 × 15	59	56		—	—		—	—		—	—		82	60		—	—	
5 × 20	—	—		—	—		—	—		—	—		—	—		—	—	
10 × 10	126	77		137	97		125	85		—	77		105	75		106	79	
10 × 15	152	115		151	130		160	95		—	88		139	93		129	96	
10 × 20	180	135		181	137		185	120		—	110		169	126		168	125	
10 × 25	—	—		241	150		—	150		—	120		—	146		—	165	
10 × 30	—	155		255	210		300	170		—	—		—	164		—	195	
10 × 40	—	—		—	—		—	—		—	—		—	—		—	270	
10 × 50	—	—		—	—		—	—		—	—		—	—		—	—	
15 × 20	—	—		—	—		300	—		—	—		—	171		—	—	
15 × 25	—	—		—	—		—	—		—	—		—	193		—	—	
15 × 40	—	—		—	—		—	—		—	—		—	—		—	—	
20 × 15	—	—		—	—		—	—		—	—		—	—		—	—	
20 × 20	—	—		—	—		—	245		—	—		—	—		—	—	
20 × 25	—	—		—	—		—	—		—	—		—	—		—	—	
20 × 30	—	—		—	—		—	—		—	—		—	—		—	—	
20 × 40	—	—		—	—		—	—		—	—		—	—		—	—	
30 × 30	—	—		—	—		—	—		—	—		—	—		—	—	

Supply Survey Results

Twelve facilities were surveyed to obtain information on current rents, occupancy levels, and market trends. Storage operators in the north and northeast submarkets indicated varying performance results, with occupancies ranging from 72% to 94%. The average occupancy level is 81%. Nine of the 12 competing projects reported increasing occupancy levels; only three reported decreasing occupancy levels.

The subject property will compete directly with Property 11 and Property 12. Both are newer properties that opened in 1998 and both struggled to reach stabilized occupancy. The extended lease-up period required for these projects is attributable to the significant increase in supply between 1997 and 2001. As of the date of the survey, both properties reported stabilized occupancies, which suggests that both properties have captured a reasonable share of market demand. Trends in occupancy levels among the competing facilities are summarized in Table 5.4.

New Supply

The market research indicates that no new facilities are planned within the immediate market area. The impact of new supply can be a significant threat to self-storage performance because the typical lease term is month to month and occupancy shifts can occur in a relatively short time. As a result, both existing and potential demand in the market must be analyzed to forecast the performance of the subject facility.

Table 5.4   Occupancy Trends

Property No.	Occupancy in 1997	Occupancy in 2001	% Change	Change in Sq. Ft.	Year Built
1	63%	72%	9	+7,874	1987, 1995
2	70%	76%	6	+1,835	1985
3	85%	73%	−12	−5,818	1988
4	85%	83%	−2	−508	1990
5	90%	80%	−10	−3,830	1964
6	65%	87%	22	+15,453	1996
7	70%	80%	10	+4,000	1995-1996
8	75%	92%	17	+11,050	1996
9	0%	80%	80	+55,920	1997
10	72%	94%	22	+3,872	1984/1996
11	0%	81%	81	+42,120	1998
12	0%	77%	77	+46,200	1998
Total net sq. ft. in market				178,168	

Demand

In this market, storage space appeals to both commercial and residential users. The typical residential user needs additional household storage or needs temporary storage while relocating; the typical commercial user is a vending route driver or sales professional. Typically, self-storage owners do not permit contractor businesses to operate in their facilities.

The subject site is located in a densely populated suburban submarket of Indianapolis. The managers of competing properties have indicated that the subject submarket is primarily a residential user market. The typical tenant mix among the competing facilities is approximately 80% residential and 20% commercial. The subject is ideally positioned to capture residential demand and the tenant mix for the subject property is projected to be 80% residential and 20% commercial.

Demonstrated Demand and Absorption

Occupancies in the market demonstrate the demand for self storage. As previously noted, the average occupancy level of the 12 identified competitors was 81% and three-fourths of the competing projects reported increasing occupancy levels.

Between 1997 and 1999 net absorption rates for properties located in the north and northeast suburban Indianapolis submarkets ranged from 1,500 to 2,500 square feet per month. Based on an average unit size of 100 square feet, the rate of absorption is 15 to 25 storage units per month. In 2000 absorption was mostly flat, with moderate fluctuations. Typically, rates of absorption are not constant in all portions of a market. Some facilities have superior locations or features, which usually indicate an above-average performance. The recent performance of new facilities in a submarket provides a measure of demonstrated demand. Details on the newest facilities in the subject's submarket and their respective absorption histories are summarized in Table 5.5.

Table 5.5 reveals that projects opening between 1995 and 1997 reported net absorption rates ranging from 966 to 4,388 square feet per month, or 2% to 11% of their net rentable area per month. Projects opening between 1998 and 2000 reported net absorption rates ranging from 824 to 2,027 square feet per month, or 2% to 4% of the facility's net rentable area per month.

Overall, the data suggests that facilities built between 1995 and 2000 had average absorption rates of 2% to 4% of the net rentable area per month. Most industry participants believe that 3% net absorption per month is a reasonable target. If a 60,000-sq.-ft. facility has a stabilized occupancy rate of 90%, then 54,000 square feet must be fully leased to achieve stabilized occupancy. To project a reasonable lease-up period, the net rentable area of 60,000 square feet is multiplied by 3% to calculate the monthly absorption rate ($60,000 \times 0.03 = 1,800$). Then the amount of space that must be leased to reach stabilized occupancy (54,000 square feet) is divided by the monthly absorption rate (1,800 square feet) to indicate the lease-up period, which in this example is 30 months, or 2.5 years.

Table 5.5 Self-Storage Absorption

1995 through 1997 Openings

	Property	Size (in Sq. Ft.)	Location Rating	Building Type	Date Opened	Average Monthly Net Absorption (in Sq. Ft.)	Monthly Lease-Up
1	Safer Self Storage 1265 Careful Drive Fishers (NE)	69,900	Good	Concrete	March 1997	3,000	4%
2	Save It Storage 370 Breaker Drive Indianapolis (N)	70,240	Good	Brick	May 1996	2,647	4%
3	The Storage Place 133 Park Drive Fishers (NE)	40,000	Average	Brick	May 1995	966	2%
4	A Storage Place 2345 Main Street Indianapolis (N)	65,000	Good	Masonry	April 1996	2,708	4%
5	Store-n-Leave 4800 Swan Road Indianapolis (SW)	39,000	Good	Brick	June 1997	4,388	11%
6	Able Self Storage 600 North Lyndon Drive Indianapolis (W)	36,000	Good	Metal	Dec. 1995	2,750	8%

1998 through 2000 Openings

	Property	Size (in Sq. Ft.)	Location Rating	Building Type	Date Opened	Average Monthly Net Absorption (in Sq. Ft.)	Monthly Lease-Up
1	Central Storage 100 Central Parkway Indianapolis (N)	65,000	Good	Masonry	June 1999	2,027	3%
2	Storage Stop 450 East Market Street Indianapolis (N)	45,000	Good	Masonry	March 2000	1,738	4%
3	Storage Unlimited 1122 22nd Street Indianapolis (E)	36,000	Average	Masonry	June 1999	824	2%
4	More Secure Self Storage 1212 Deer Run Road Indianapolis (NE)	52,000	Good	Masonry	June 1998	1,000	2%

Based on the preceding analysis, a projected absorption rate of 2% to 4% of net rentable area per month appears reasonable for the subject property. Now that demand has been demonstrated for the existing facilities, future demand must be considered.

Potential Demand

To measure potential demand, an estimate of the average rentable square feet (RSF) of storage space per person will be applied to the current population in the identified market area. The results are compared to the existing storage supply to measure the balance of supply and demand. This type of projection is never perfect since storage markets overlap, but it does reveal some basic supply/demand relationships.

As noted in the analysis of existing supply, the average rentable square feet (RSF) of storage space per person has increased in recent years to approximately 4.0 in several secondary Midwestern cities. It has also increased throughout the State of Indiana. To project overall storage demand in the subject's submarket, the 4.00 RSF, which is considered reasonable for the market area, is multiplied by the population living within a three-mile radius of the subject property. The calculations are shown below.

So, given the 2000 population of 30,711, the potential demand for storage space is 122,844 square feet. Given the projected population of 35,197 in 2005, the potential demand for storage space is estimated at 140,788 square feet. Based on this analysis, the total submarket storage need is calculated at approximately 123,000 to 141,000 square feet over the next four years.

The survey of properties in the north and northeast Indianapolis submarkets (Table 5.3) included 12 properties with a total net rentable area of approximately 605,000 square feet. While it appears there is an oversupply of storage space in this market, it is important to note that many of these properties do not directly compete with the subject property. This large sample of properties was surveyed merely to accumulate market data with which to quantify market conditions in the region and develop a market rent estimate.

Reviewing the map of competing facilities in Figure 5.4 reveals that most of the surveyed properties are located along major thoroughfares or off the freeway. The subject property is located on a secondary street in a mostly residential area. Property 11 is near the subject property and has a comparable location profile. This property is also relatively new. Interviews with its management indicate that this is the most comparable facility in the market.

Property 12 is the next most competitive property. It is near to the subject, is relatively new, and appears to anchor the northern portion of the submarket. Although Property 4, at the southern end of the submarket, appears to be competitive with the subject property, it is not. This property is influenced by different neighborhood demographics and does not benefit from the established traffic patterns of

	Population	RSF per Person	Storage Need
2000	30,711 ×	4.00 =	122,844
2005*	35,197 ×	4.00 =	140,788

* Projected

the northeast neighborhoods. The properties located on the edge of the submarket (Properties 2, 3, and 5) do not compete directly with the subject property, but they are influential in eliminating potential demand in the northwest section of the submarket. They represent secondary competition. Although the properties outside the submarket are not competitive with the subject property, they can be used to demonstrate area rental rates and occupancy trends.

Properties 11 and 12 are directly competitive with the subject property. The secondary competitors along the freeway represent approximately 117,000 square feet of storage area, but only 20% of this space should be allocated to the subject submarket. Table 5.6 shows the influence of the two primary competitors and the secondary competitors in the subject submarket. The proposed subject property is also shown.

Table 5.6 Submarket Supply and Demand

	Size (in Sq. Ft.)	× Occupancy	=	Leased Area (in Sq. Ft.)	Projected Available Supply (Vacancy)
Property 11	52,000	81%		42,120	9,880
Property 12	60,000	77%		46,200	13,800
Secondary supply Properties 2, 3 & 5 (117,355 × 20%)	23,471	75%		17,603	5,868
Submarket total	135,471			105,923	29,548
Subject property	61,300	0%		0	61,300

The potential storage demand was estimated to range from 123,000 to 141,000 square feet over the next four years. The current supply indicates that 135,471 square feet have already been absorbed, suggesting that the market is satisfied without the addition of the subject property. The current data indicates the subject project is not feasible.

Since population growth is moderate, the generation of new demand is also moderate. The existing properties in this submarket will compete for transient residential business and a limited amount of commercial business. Market demand was low in 2000 and expected to remain flat in 2001. Based on the survey of absorption rates, the two primary competitors could potentially have net lease-up gains of 500 to 800 square feet per month, or 6,000 to 9,600 square feet per year.

This rate of absorption is quite low. The low absorption rate, combined with nominal capture by the secondary competitors, indicates that all these properties will compete heavily for market capture. Simply put, these facilities must not only lease space to fill current vacancies, they also face typical tenant attrition, which will add to the supply of vacant space. This is one reason why self storage is a tough business. When supply exceeds demand, it inevitably leads to rental rate concessions, which lead to lower-than-expected financial performance. If the subject property were built, it would likely capture a fair share of the demand that is now shared by the two primary competitors. This would result in occupancy rates of about 50% for the three primary competitors. The current rate of absorption would guarantee low occupancy levels until 2005 or beyond.

Another Scenario—Feasible Project

The remainder of the case study will be based on the information contained in this portion of the example. For this analysis, it is assumed that Property 12 does not exist. The new submarket supply profile is shown in Table 5.7.

Table 5.7 New Submarket Supply and Demand

	Size (in Sq. Ft.)	× Occupancy	=	Leased Area (in Sq. Ft.)	Projected Available Supply (Vacancy)
Property 11	52,000	81%		42,120	9,880
Secondary supply Properties 2,3, &5 (117,355 × 20%)	23,471	75%		17,603	5,868
Submarket total	75,471			59,723	15,748
Subject property	61,300	0%		0	61,300

Based on these new assumptions, the immediate submarket has a total supply of 75,471 square feet of storage space and potential demand for 123,000 to 141,000 square feet. The market is now underserved. If the subject property were built, the supply would increase to 136,771 square feet, which can clearly be supported based on the market research, which indicates that the market has pent-up demand.

Pent-Up Demand and Initial Lease-Up

In this new scenario, with one of the competitive properties eliminated, the subject submarket has pent-up demand due to a lack of facilities. In reality, if there was a significant amount of pent-up demand in a market, the existing competitors would report occupancy levels higher than 95% and a waiting list for certain types of units.

For the purpose of this analysis and to develop a cash flow analysis, a typical absorption period based on area performance rates will be estimated for the subject. If the property were in high demand, there would likely be a spike in leasing for the first few months followed by a leveling off of demand after the unsatisfied demand was satisfied. The subject property has 61,300 rentable square feet and can achieve an estimated net absorption of 1,500 to 2,000 square feet per month over the next few years, assuming that no new supply is added. Based on a stabilized occupancy rate of 90%, or 55,260 square feet, the required absorption period ranges from 28 to 37 months. For this analysis, the absorption period is estimated to be three years. Based on the estimated rate of absorption, the subject property will lease approximately 18,420 square feet of space per year in the first three years of operation.

Most of the facilities surveyed have climate-controlled storage space, which is now standard in newer developments. Generally 20% to 30% of the facility's net rentable area is allocated to climate-controlled units. Approximately 33% of the proposed subject development will be allocated to climate-controlled units. Climate-controlled space is typically more expensive than regular storage space and such space is available at other facilities in the submarket. This space is likely to lease at a similar rate as the entire project. Thus, it can be assumed that all space will be leased to a 90% occupancy level at the end of the three-year period.

Rental Rate Analysis

Table 5.8 shows projected rental rates for the subject property based on the rental rate data of the properties surveyed. The rent analysis included both climate-controlled and regular storage units of various sizes. After reviewing the average market rates, the appraiser can estimate market rents for each of the unit types at the subject property. The rents are then converted into a gross income estimate for the subject property.

Market Position of the Subject Property

The subject property will be located in a residential area that is somewhat isolated from major roadways. The property will have the advantage of being one of only two competitors in a submarket that appears to have a shortage of space. The competitors at the edge of the submarket will likely experience some loss of business when the subject property opens since the subject is strategically positioned near the housing base of the region. The subject property is a typical Class B facility with regular and climate-controlled space. While market conditions suggest that the broader economy may be in recession, the subject submarket is growing and seems undersupplied. In terms of investment potential, the subject property fits the criteria of many national and regional investors. The property has a functional mix of units and appealing elements such as an on-site manager's apartment and concrete block construction. The subject property should capture a reasonable share of market demand.

Highest and Best Use

The market value of any property is a function of its highest and best use. The highest and best use of a property is the reasonably probable and legal use which is physically possible, appropriately supported in the market, financially feasible, and results in the highest value.

Table 5.8 Income Projection for Falls River Self Storage

Unit Type	No. of Units	Unit Size (in Sq. Ft.)	Total Area (in Sq. Ft.)	Monthly Market Rent	Unit Rent/ Sq. Ft.	Monthly Gross Potential Income (*GPI*)	Annual Gross Potential Income (*GPI*)
5 × 5	11	25	275	$40	$1.60	$440	$5,280
5 × 5 (C)*	28	25	700	$50	$2.00	$1,400	$16,800
5 × 10	38	50	1,900	$50	$1.00	$1,900	$22,800
5 × 10 (C)	70	50	3,500	$75	$1.50	$5,250	$63,000
5 × 15	17	75	1,275	$70	$0.93	$1,190	$14,280
10 × 10	76	100	7,600	$80	$0.80	$6,080	$72,960
10 × 10 (C)	86	100	8,600	$110	$1.10	$9,460	$113,520
10 × 15	56	150	8,400	$95	$0.63	$5,320	$63,840
10 × 15 (C)	27	150	4,050	$130	$0.87	$3,510	$42,120
10 × 20	62	200	12,400	$120	$0.60	$7,440	$89,280
10 × 20 (C)	13	200	2,600	$160	$0.80	$2,080	$24,960
10 × 25	8	250	2,000	$135	$0.54	$1,080	$12,960
10 × 25 (C)	2	250	500	$160	$0.64	$320	$3,840
10 × 30	14	300	4,200	$155	$0.52	$2,170	$26,040
10 × 40	1	400	400	$200	$0.50	$200	$2,400
15 × 20	2	300	600	$160	$0.53	$320	$3,840
20 × 25	1	500	500	$245	$0.49	$245	$2,940
20 × 30	3	600	1,800	$300	$0.50	$900	$10,800
Total	515		61,300			$49,305	$591,660
Total climate-controlled area			19,950				
Total other storage area			41,350				
Total			61,300				
Average annual rent/sq. ft. heated	$13.25						
Average annual rent/sq. ft. unheated	$7.92						

* C identifies climate-controlled space

Analysis of the highest and best use of the subject property involves consideration of the site as though vacant and available for development and the property as improved with the proposed improvements.

Site as Though Vacant

The site is a 4.5-acre rectangular parcel with significant frontage and depth. Many uses are physically possible and legal, but the financially feasible uses are dictated by the balance between supply and demand in the market. Market analysis and income analysis indicate that the proposed self-storage project is a feasible use that maximizes the productivity of the site and will generate significant net income. The self-storage project should conform to local zoning restrictions and be developed with the same quality and configuration as other successful facilities in the area.

Site as Improved

The proposed improvements are physically possible and legal and they maximize the value of the site. It has been demonstrated through market analysis and income analysis that the proposed project is financially feasible. The proposed unit configuration is appropriate and the facility will have curb appeal, which will add to its overall marketability.

Income Analysis

The appraiser applies the income capitalization approach to estimate value based on the amount of net income the property will generate. When discounted cash flow analysis is used, the market value of the property is estimated by discounting the projected income stream over an anticipated holding period. The reversionary value is estimated by capitalizing the last year's net operating income with a terminal capitalization rate, thus reflecting an assumed sale of the property at the end of the holding period. The resulting cash flows and reversionary value are discounted at a rate that reflects the durability, timing, and risk of the cash flow in comparison to alternative investments.

Rental Income

The base rental income is the income received from the rental of heated and unheated storage units. In market analysis the appraiser estimates market rent, which forms the basis for projecting base rental income. In light of current market conditions, which are very competitive, rate increases of 0% in Year 1 and 1% per year thereafter are estimated.

Other Income

In most self-storage properties, other income is generated by imposing administrative fees, late fees, and NSF charges and by selling locks and packaging materials. Within the industry, the typical ratio for other income is 2.5% of effective gross income. This percentage can vary greatly depending on the property. A well-planned retail display area can generate sales that exceed 9% of effective gross income. A truck rental operation can generate increased traffic and result in higher sales. Conversely, a rural facility with no office may generate small amounts of other income. The subject property has a large office with a retail display area so other income for the subject is estimated to be 6% of effective gross income.

Vacancy and Collection Loss

The occupancy levels of the competing properties ranged from 72% to 94%. Based on interviews with area managers, the losses due to collection problems are nominal in this submarket. Considering the position of the proposed subject property, a combined vacancy and collection loss of 10% is considered reasonable. This amount is deducted from effective gross rental income.

Estimated Operating Expenses

The subject's operating expenses are estimated and described in the following paragraphs.

Advertising. This expense includes fees for Yellow Pages advertising and other forms of marketing. Based on local costs, a first-year expense of $7,000 is reasonable. This equates to an expense of $0.12 per square foot, which is lower than the estimated average cost of $0.26 per square foot. The size of the Yellow Pages ad and the amount of other advertising will affect this expense.

Administrative. This category includes a wide variety of office/administrative expenses such as the cost of telephone service, supplies, professional fees, and postage. The first-year expense is estimated to be $17,000, or $0.28 per square foot; this is comparable to the industry average of $0.26 per square foot.

Staff salaries & benefits. National statistics indicate that this expense generally ranges from $15,000 to $30,000. This estimate is low and these expenses typically vary by market. A typical 60,000-sq.-ft. facility requires one full-time manager and a part-time assistant. For this analysis, a first-year expense of $48,000 is estimated.

Management fee. In this market, management fees for self-storage facilities range from 4% to 5% of effective gross income. For the subject property, a management fee of 5% of effective gross income *(EGI)* will be used.

Utilities. The utility expense covers water, electricity, gas, and trash removal. The highest cost is for heating and cooling the climate-controlled units. A first-year expense of $12,500 is estimated.

Repairs and maintenance. This category includes snow removal in addition to typical repair and maintenance items. The facility is new, so minimal repair and maintenance will be needed. The first-year expense is estimated to be $7,000.

Insurance. Statistics suggest an expense of $4,000 to $5,000 for insurance. Based on local costs, a first-year expense of $9,000 is estimated.

Real estate taxes. The first-year tax expense will be approximately $74,000.

Reserves. A reasonable reserve allowance for the subject is estimated to be $0.05 per square foot, or $3,000 for the replacement of short-lived components.

A complete cash flow projection for the subject property is shown in Table 5.9.

Table 5.9 Cash Flow Projection

Absorption		Year 1 Ending Dec. 31 2004	Year 2 Ending Dec. 31 2005	Stabilized Year 3 Ending Dec. 31 2006	Year 4 Reversion 2007
Total proposed size in sq. ft.— unheated space		41,350	13,783	27,567	41,350	41,350
Total proposed size in sq. ft.— heated space		19,950	6,650	13,300	19,950	19,950
Total facility size (sq. ft.)		61,300	20,433	40,867	61,300	61,300
Total lease-up (starts at 0)						
Per month average			1,703	1,703	1,703	
Unheated storage space market rent per sq. ft.	$7.92					
Heated storage space market rent per sq. ft.	$13.25					
Income						
Gross storage income			$197,217	$394,443	$591,660	$591,660
Income rate increase = 0, 1%, 1%, 1%			$0	$3,944	$3,984	$5,956
Less vacancy & collection loss			$0	$0	$59,564	$59,762
Effective gross income (*EGI*)			$197,217	$398,387	$536,080	$537,854
Other income @ 6% of *EGI*			11,833	23,903	32,165	32,271
Total *EGI*:			$209,050	$422,290	$568,245	$570,125
Expenses						
Advertising			$7,000	$7,210	$7,426	$7,649
Administrative			17,000	17,510	18,035	18,576
Manager's salary & benefits			48,000	49,440	50,923	52,451
Management fee @ 5% of *EGI*			9,861	19,919	26,804	26,893
Utilities			12,500	12,875	13,261	13,659
Repairs and maintenance			7,000	7,210	7,426	7,649
Insurance			9,000	9,270	9,548	9,835
Real estate taxes			74,000	74,000	74,000	74,000
Reserves			3,000	3,000	3,000	3,000
Less total expenses			$187,361	$200,434	$210,423	$213,712
Net operating income			$21,690	$221,856	$357,822	$356,413

* Climate-controlled

Discounted Cash Flow Analysis

The discounted cash flow methodology is used to estimate the present value of the income stream and the reversion. The projected income and expenses over the holding period are estimated to yield annual cash flow. The reversion value is equal to the Year 3 *NOI* capitalized at a terminal capitalization rate minus a sales commission. The annual cash flow estimates and reversion are discounted at an appropriate rate, which reflects the risk, durability, and timing of the income stream relative to alternative investments available in the market.

Derivation of Overall Capitalization Rate

An overall capitalization rate is estimated based on industry surveys, available statistics, and rates extracted from sales data. Table 5.10 summarizes a group of hypothetical sales and illustrates the derivation of an overall rate for each transaction.

Table 5.10 Derivation of Overall Rates

	Sale 1	Sale 2	Sale 3	Sale 4
Sale price	$1,700,000	$1,200,000	$1,450,000	$1,900,000
Effective gross income	$250,000	$170,000	$200,000	$275,000
Expenses	$88,500	$50,000	$58,625	$85,000
Expense ratio	35%	29%	29%	31%
Net operating income (*NOI*)	$161,500	$120,000	$141,375	$190,000
OAR (R_o)	9.5%	10.0%	9.8%	10.0%

Published data can suggest an appropriate rate. The *Self Storage Almanac* lists more than 250 self-storage sales that occurred in the United States between 1995 and 2000. The capitalization rates of the sales ranged from 8% to 12%, with an average rate of 10.27%.

The investor survey in the most recent issue of the *Korpacz Real Estate Investment Survey* published by PriceWaterhouseCoopers was consulted. The survey is a special report for the national self-storage market. This survey indicates residual cap rates in the range of 10% to 10.5% for storage properties and discusses going-in rates of 10% to 11%. The survey also points out that discount rates for storage range from 13% to 14% with 3% to 3.5% rental rate growth. The low rental growth rate of 0% to 1% for the subject calls for a lower discount rate.

Given the property's position in the market and the risks associated with the location and configuration, a direct and reversionary capitalization rate of 10% has been estimated. This rate is used to capitalize the stabilized net income.

Discount Rate

Considering the previous investor survey, a discount rate of approximately 12%, or 2% over the going-in capitalization rate, is estimated.

Reversion Value

The reversion value is calculated by capitalizing the *NOI* in the fourth year of the projection period by the terminal capitalization rate of 10%. The costs of sale, which are estimated at 3% of the sale price in the reversion year, are then deducted to produce a final net reversion value. The future value of the property is calculated below using the rates selected.

Year 4 *NOI* (2007)	$356,414
Divided by R_o	10%
Gross reversion value	$3,564,140
Less costs of sale @ 3%	− $106,924
Net reversion value	$3,457,216

Value Conclusion by the Income Approach—Upon Completion—at Present Value

Table 5.11 summarizes the present value of the cash flows and reversion.

Using discounted cash flow analysis, the market value of the subject property upon completion is estimated to be $2,910,000.

Table 5.11 Present Value at Completion

12% = Discount rate
10% = Terminal cap rate

Period	No. of Months	Year	Cash Flow	Present Value Factor*	Present Value Amount
1	12	2001	$21,690	0.8929	$19,366
2	24	2002	$221,856	0.7972	$176,862
3	36	2003	$357,820	0.7118	$254,689
Reversion	36	2003	$3,457,219	0.7118	$2,460,780
				Net present value	$2,911,697
				Rounded	$2,910,000
				Value per sq. ft. of NRA	$47.47

* Rounded

Direct Capitalization—Upon Stabilization—Prospective Future Value

Table 5.12 is the stabilized operating statement for the subject property.

Table 5.12   Stabilized Operating Statement

Falls River Self Storage

Income		Dollars per Sq. Ft. NRA	% of EGI
Gross potential rental income—stabilized	$591,660	9.65	
Plus rent increases	$3,984		
Less vacancy & collection loss @ 10%	59,564	0.97	
Effective gross rental income (*EGI*)	$536,080	8.75	
Other income @ 6%	$32,165	0.52	
Total effective income	$568,245	9.27	100
Expenses			
Advertising	$7,426	0.12	1
Administrative	$18,035	0.29	3
Manager's salary & benefits	$50,923	0.83	9
Management fee @ 5% of *EGI*	$26,804	0.44	5
Utilities	$13,261	0.22	2
Repairs and maintenance	$7,426	0.12	1
Insurance	$9,548	0.16	2
Real estate taxes	$74,000	1.21	13
Reserves	$3,000	0.05	1
Less total expenses	$210,423	$3.44	37%
Net operating income	$357,822	$5.84*	63%
Expense ratio			37%

* Rounded

Direct Capitalization—Upon Stabilization—Future Value

Capitalization is the process of converting a series of anticipated future periodic installments of net income into present value. The estimated prospective market value for the subject property is calculated by dividing the estimated stabilized net operating income of $357,822 by the selected overall capitalization rate of 10%.

$357,822/10% = $3,578,220, or $3,580,000 (rounded)

Financial Feasibility

Table 5.13 shows the budgeted costs for the project. These costs are not necessarily typical, especially the lease-up expenses, but they can be used as a basis for evaluating feasibility.

Table 5.13 Cost Breakdown—Falls River Self Storage

Hard Costs	Cost
Land	$530,944
Buildings	$1,575,000
Security/monitor system	$30,165
Office setup	$12,400
Total hard costs	$2,148,509
Soft Costs	
Loan fees	$63,750
Legal fees	$15,000
Title insurance	$4,000
Appraisal	$5,000
Architect/engineering	$42,038
Environmental	$1,700
Development/consulting fees	$150,000
Surveys	$4,000
Loan interest	$80,000
Closing costs	$2,000
Contingency	$75,000
Lease-up expenses	$240,000
Total soft costs	$682,488
Total construction budget	**$2,830,997**

The project has a budget of approximately $2,831,000. As previously indicated, the present value of the project is $2,910,000, confirming that the development is financially feasible. If the present value were less than the actual costs, then the project would not be financially feasible.